THE MUSLIM QUESTION IN CANADA

THE MUSLIM QUESTION IN CANADA

A STORY OF SEGMENTED INTEGRATION

Abdolmohammad Kazemipur

UBCPress · Vancouver · Toronto

22 21 20 19 18 17 16 15 14   5 4 3 2 1

Printed in Canada on FSC-certified ancient-forest-free paper
(100% post-consumer recycled) that is processed chlorine- and acid-free.

Library and Archives Canada Cataloguing in Publication

Kazemipur, Abdolmohammad, author
    The Muslim question in Canada : a story of segmented integration /
Abdolmohammad Kazemipur.

Includes bibliographical references and index.
Issued in print and electronic formats.
ISBN 978-0-7748-2729-4 (bound). – ISBN 978-0-7748-2730-0 (pbk.). –
ISBN 978-0-7748-2731-7 (pdf). – ISBN 978-0-7748-2732-4 (epub)

    1. Muslims – Cultural assimilation – Canada. 2. Muslims – Canada – Social conditions. 3. Muslims – Canada – Economic conditions. 4. Immigrants – Canada – Social conditions. 5. Immigrants – Canada – Economic conditions. 6. Canada – Emigration and immigration – Social aspects. 7. Canada – Ethnic relations. I. Title.

FC106.M9K39 2014   305.6'970971   C2014-901962-9
                                                        C2014-901963-7

Canadä

UBC Press gratefully acknowledges the financial support for our publishing program of the Government of Canada (through the Canada Book Fund), the Canada Council for the Arts, and the British Columbia Arts Council.

This book has been published with the help of a grant from the Canadian Federation for the Humanities and Social Sciences, through the Awards to Scholarly Publications Program, using funds provided by the Social Sciences and Humanities Research Council of Canada.

UBC Press
The University of British Columbia
2029 West Mall
Vancouver, BC V6T 1Z2
www.ubcpress.ca

Contents

Figures and Tables

Tables

Preface

This book serves as a partial response to an existential question with which I have been grappling since my arrival in Canada, about twenty years ago, from Iran, a Muslim-majority country. Faced with the enormous challenge of settling in a country one ocean and two continents away from my homeland, whose language I did not speak and with whose customs and culture I was not familiar, I started looking for anyone with whom I could find the slightest commonality. That naturally brought me into contact with Iranian expatriates, but it also brought me into contact with various circles of Muslims, from international students to established citizens, from Shia Muslims to Sunnis and Ismailis, and from Europeans to Arabs to South and East Asians. Those contacts drove home to me the enormous diversity of beliefs and practices within Canadian Muslims, and it triggered an interest not only in learning more about how they manage such diversity but also about how they reconcile their faith with life in a non-Muslim-majority country and how they are perceived by the non-Muslims around them. In search of answers to these questions, I started compiling data and accumulating my observations, but only casually and unsystematically.

And then the 9/11 tragedy happened. Overnight, I saw that the questions that lurked in the dark corners of my mind were now marching on the silver screen of my TV. In a strange way, that was a little reassuring as I felt that those questions had not been just the products of my particular ignorance; or that, if ignorance was at work, it was widely shared (which always makes one feel better). While it was comforting to hear others asking the same questions, it was not comforting to hear the answers that a small number of TV pundits were providing. Their answers, I felt, were greatly oversimplified, partial, and full of personal bias. No less important, they did not match my casual observations.

As I was listening to some Muslim-bashing TV reports, for example, two contingents of neighbours showed up at our door, each offering caring and support in its own special way. The first, a nice family of devout Christians, offered us a kind letter, reassuring us that they saw us as good neighbours and friends and that the 9/11 events would not affect our friendly relationship. The second, a middle-aged single woman with Aboriginal roots, offered us a decorative candle and the marvellous gift of an eagle feather that she had kept since her childhood years. Upon leaving, she also advised us to store a few sacks of potato and bags of flour, just to be prepared for "the imminent war." These nice gestures were not compatible with the angry anti-Muslim voices I was hearing in the mass media.

As is always the case, a question is born every time things do not easily add up or when observations do not match expectations. In this case, my personal observations and expectations were in conflict with the arguments that were increasingly presented in the media. Something was definitely missing, and this led me to study the issue further, in a more comprehensive and systematic way. And this is what I did over the next decade, first as a side project but later, since 2009, as a main line of activity. This book is the first print product of that work.

As in the case of any other research-based product, the preparation of this book benefitted greatly from the work, assistance, and support of many people and organizations. First and foremost, I would like to acknowledge the high-quality work of my research assistants, who helped in various stages of the study: Natasha Fairweather, Christopher Birrell, Taha Azizi, Martin Russenberger, Maede Ejaredar, Osman Shah, and Kathy Fitzpatrick. I would also like to acknowledge the assistance of my colleague, Dr. Willow Anderson, for her careful reading of the manuscript and her great suggestions for changes.

The financial support for this project was provided by the Social Sciences and Humanities Research Council of Canada, the Metropolis Project, the University of Lethbridge, and Memorial University of Newfoundland. The last part of my work on this book coincided with my appointment as the Stephen Jarislowsky Chair in Culture Change at Memorial University. I acknowledge the support I received through the resources available to me through this position. This book is published with the help of a grant from the Federation for the Humanities and Social Sciences, through the Awards to Scholarly Publications Program, using funds provided by the Social Science and Humanities Research Council of Canada.

A big chunk of the data used in this book has come from the master files of the surveys conducted by Statistics Canada, made available through Statistics Canada's research data centres (RDCs). The RDC initiative provides researchers with something close to a gold mine, and for this it deserves to be commended. Of course, the views expressed, and possible errors in data analysis, are all mine, and the above organizations have no responsibility in this regard.

Colleagues at UBC Press went beyond my expectations in pushing this book through the publication process. From the initial conversation about doing a project like this, through arranging the peer-review process, to securing financial support and, finally, the production of the book, everything was conducted with rigour, professionalism, and high standards. I would like to particularly thank Emily Andrew, Holly Keller, and Joanne Richardson for their great work on this project.

Last, but not least, I owe a great debt to my family, both the extended and the immediate, and, in particular, to my wife and our two sons. Every page of this book is a chunk of my time denied to them – a time that could have been spent in making their lives easier and more pleasant. I am hoping that, by making a small contribution to the understanding and, perhaps, to the betterment of the world in which we live, this book can partially make up for my not having spent more time with them.

THE MUSLIM QUESTION IN CANADA

1

Introduction

In his controversial book entitled *The Clash of Civilizations*, Samuel Huntington (1996) predicts that conflicts between Muslims and non-Muslims will start to rise all over the world. Proposing a conceptual framework for understanding the post-Cold War world, he suggests that global conflicts will no longer be driven by ideological convictions but, rather, by cultural affiliations. The new fault lines, according to him, are going to be found not between countries with different political ideologies – such as Marxism/capitalism – but between relatively homogenous cultural blocks. This new dynamic is expected to create two types of conflicts: (1) inter-civilizational at the global level and (2) inter-ethnic at the local level. The emerging cultural/civilizational blocks, according to Huntington, are African, Japanese, Orthodox (Russian), Islamic, Western, Hindu, and Sinic (Chinese); and the relationship between each pair of civilizations could vary from non-existent to "less conflictual" to "more conflictual." In his view, the Islamic civilization is in a class of its own in that four of the five relationships it has with other civilizations are "more conflictual" (Huntington 1996, 245). So the tensions between Muslims and non-Muslims are expected to escalate everywhere in the years to come. And, indeed, many developments after 1996 seemed to confirm this expectation.

However, Huntington's thesis revolves mostly around nations and historically shaped ethnic minorities, not immigrant communities. Huntington discusses such communities only marginally, a fact reflected in his allocating fewer than ten pages to a discussion of the place of immigration in this newly emerging world. In these pages, he acknowledges the presence of an "immigrant invasion" on both sides of the Atlantic – with a Hispanic/ Mexican invasion in the United States and an Arab/Muslim invasion in Europe. However, he treats the former as tentative and uncertain, and the latter as declining. Regarding the latter, he writes: "The problem of Muslim demographic invasion is ... likely to weaken as the population growth rates in North African and Middle Eastern societies peak, as they already have in some countries, and begin to decline ... Muslim immigration could be much less by 2025 ... and the threat to Europe of 'Islamization' will be succeeded by that of 'Africanization'" (Huntington 1996, 204). This prediction is in clear contrast to the situation on both sides of the Atlantic today. In the almost two decades since Huntington wrote those lines, not only did the issue of Muslim immigration continue, even intensify, in Europe but it also emerged in North America. This issue is now the subject of one of the hottest debates of our time.

The rise of Muslim immigration as a socio-political issue during the opening decade of the twenty-first century is related to an emerging perception that the integration of Muslim immigrants into Western liberal democracies has been particularly problematic. The attacks on the Twin Towers and Pentagon on 11 September 2001 were a major trigger in this process, particularly in the United States. Shortly after, Europe witnessed a series of violent and/or terrorist events – the assassination of the Dutch film director Theo van Gogh in 2004, the Madrid train bombing in 2004, the London subway bombing in 2005, and the social unrest in France in 2005 – all of which involved individuals of Muslim backgrounds. As a consequence of these events, the already-existing European debates on Muslim immigrants greatly intensified and took on new dimensions. Later, in 2006, the arrest of eighteen terrorism suspects in Toronto brought similar concerns to Canada. The involvement of individuals of Muslim backgrounds, and the fact that many of them were second-generation immigrants, raised serious questions about the degree to which Muslim minorities could live peacefully with the native-born populations and other minorities in immigrant-receiving countries.

The reasons given for the perceived non-integration of Muslims into liberal democracies were just as influential as were the aforementioned events in turning the issue of Muslim immigration into a socio-political problem. A popular response quickly surfaced, most visibly in Europe, according to which the source of the problem was considered to be either the unwillingness or the inability of Muslim immigrants to integrate into the immigrant-receiving countries. The building blocks of this "standard" answer are: (1) Muslim immigrants tend not to integrate into host societies; (2) this is a conscious decision; (3) this decision is made because the goal of Muslim immigrants is to dominate, rather than to blend into, Western societies; and (4) there are no variations within Muslims in this regard, no extremist-moderate and no conservative-liberal distinctions (for an elaborate discussion of these views, see Saunders [2012b]).

At the heart of all this is the notion of "Muslim exceptionalism" – that is, a perceived fundamental difference between Muslim and other immigrants with regard to their interaction with host societies. By allowing the experiences of Muslim immigrants to be viewed as an exception to the rule and as something related to Muslim immigrants themselves, the resultant discourses allowed both the problem and the responsibility for resolving it to be shifted away from the host populations and towards the Muslim immigrants. This not only grossly oversimplifies a complex and multifaceted problem but also removes the possibility that the mainstream population might have to take some moral responsibility for it.

When it comes to explaining a complex socio-political problem, such oversimplifications are hardly helpful: when they begin to influence major state policies, they are clearly dangerous. And this is exactly what is happening with regard to the simplistic notion of "Muslim exceptionalism," which has influenced several major policy debates in Western Europe and North America – debates on the balance between civil liberties and security measures, on secularism, and on multiculturalism (Cesari 2005). In the latter case, while critiques of multiculturalism policies have been around since the early 1970s, they have greatly intensified since the mid-2000s, and, recently, Muslims have been at the heart of the debate. As Modood (2007, 4) points out: "Muslims have become central to the merits and demerits of Multiculturalism as a public policy." Interestingly, Kymlicka (2005) observes that the strength of the opposition to multiculturalism in various countries has been proportional to the size of their Muslim immigrant populations. In sum, in the politically correct cultural environment of many of these countries, as Kalin (2011, 4) argues, "attacks on multiculturalism have become indirect attacks on Islam and Muslims."

Canadian Multiculturalism

The debates around multiculturalism are particularly relevant for Canada as it was the first country to adopt multiculturalism as an official policy and is often referred to as a nation whose experiments with this policy have been reasonably successful (Reitz 2009a). However, despite its success story, and more than four decades of experimentation, even Canada seems to be grappling with multiculturalism. A brief historical sketch of these four decades will help us to better appreciate the implications of the current study.

Dewing (2009) presents the history of multiculturalism in Canada as occurring in three phases: (1) pre-1971, the incipient phase; (2) 1971-81, the formative phase; and (3) 1982-present, the institutionalization phase. It was in 1971 that Prime Minister Pierre Trudeau adopted the policy of multiculturalism. This was followed, in 1982, by the addition of a clause in section 27 of the Canadian Charter of Rights and Freedoms that states: "[the Charter] shall be interpreted in a manner consistent with the preservation and enhancement of the multicultural heritage of Canadians" (5). This was an important change, and it resulted in the passing of several other pieces of legislation, all of which were influenced by a new interpretation of the Charter. And this paved the way for the Canadian Multiculturalism Act, which Parliament adopted in 1988.

The process through which Canadian multiculturalism came about was not an easy one, nor was it without controversy. Trudeau's initial declaration of his multiculturalism policy, for instance, was strongly criticized by Quebec, which perceived the new legislation as having the potential to undermine the distinct status of French Canadians by treating them as one culture among many as opposed to one of two (alongside English Canadians); there were also some worries that the promotion of ethnic languages could eclipse the French language, particularly in Quebec (Reitz 2009a). The special case of Quebec aside, there were more general concerns about the degree to which an emphasis on multiculturalism might come into conflict with the three main liberal-democratic values of freedom, equality, and solidarity (Kymlicka 2010) (this set of concerns, however, arrived on the scene a little later).

Despite some scattered academic works on multiculturalism during the 1970s and 1980s, according to Kymlicka (2010), the most serious wave of scholarship on this issue began to surface in the 1990s. A hallmark of this new wave was Charles Taylor's (1992) *Multiculturalism and the Politics of Recognition*, in which he tries to provide a political-philosophical justification for the concept of multiculturalism by treating it as an essential component of one's outlook on the world and the self. In Taylor's view, society's "recognition" of one's ethnic/cultural background constitutes an essential part of one's sense of identity.

Taylor's work marks the beginning of a golden decade for the idea of multiculturalism. But, even in that golden decade, the idea did not go unchallenged. Two years after the initial publication of Taylor's work, it was republished in an expanded form, which included a few other contributions from scholars who critiqued the concept from many different angles, most of which concerned the potential conflicts between such a recognition and the fundamental values of a liberal democracy (i.e., freedom, equality, and solidarity). However, the critics were kept at bay for quite some time due to the rapid increase in the worldwide popularity of both the concept and the policy of multiculturalism during the 1980s and 1990s, as reflected in the increasing number of countries that adopted them and the growing number of legislative rulings within each country that was influenced by them.

The events of 9/11, however, triggered a new phase in the life of multiculturalism, and a new wave of critiques surfaced in academia and in the broader society. Frequent references (implicit or explicit) were now made to Muslims' being an example of why multiculturalism is not a good policy and as evidence of why it cannot work. While the issue of Muslims was never absent in the previous debates on multiculturalism, it now took centre stage.

So, in the global debates on multiculturalism, special places are occupied by Canada and by Muslims: Canada is used as evidence that multiculturalism works; Muslims are used as evidence that it does not. Given this, it is important to examine the experiences of Muslim immigrants in Canada. Such a study should serve to introduce a welcome nuance to the existing debates in the field.

The Muslim Question

The distinct place of Muslim immigrants in Western liberal democracies and the debates surrounding it comprise what I call "the Muslim question." At the heart of this question lies a perception of the uneasy relationship between Muslims and the rest, and the idea that the roots of this relationship are to be found in the cultural orientation and religious beliefs of Muslims themselves. I also use this phrase because it echoes "the Jewish question," bringing to mind the similarities between the experiences of Muslim immigrants today and those of Jewish minorities in late-nineteenth-century Europe (for a similar adoption of this concept, see Norton, 2013).

The Jewish question was constituted by a perception among Christian populations in Europe that people of the Jewish faith – particularly those originating from Eastern Europe – comprised a distinct group, whose perceived defining features were very similar to those listed for Muslim immigrants today. According to Saunders (2012b, 129), it was believed that Eastern European Jewish immigrants maintained "strange and conservative religious customs and seemed determined not to integrate"; that they were "potential threats" and were "associated with criminality and violence" – so much so that "the new immigrants' dark clothes and head coverings soon became emblems of civilizational conflict." Later, this perceived civilizational and cultural distinction was combined with a perceived tendency to embrace political radicalism and extremist platforms. According to Saunders, the image of the Jew had become that of "an impossible-to-assimilate outsider ... a key backer of radicalism and violent revolution" (134). The strong similarities between the experiences of Jews in late-nineteenth-century Europe and those of Muslims today is well captured by Huntington (1996, 200): "In Western Europe, anti-Semitism directed against Arabs has largely replaced anti-Semitism directed against Jews."

To what extent is the Muslim question a Canadian issue? This is an important question because, as mentioned earlier, Canada is often viewed as a country whose unique experiences make it a model when it comes to issues concerning the immigration system, the integration of immigrants, ethnic diversity, and multiculturalism. This is frequently mentioned by researchers in the field, both Canadian and non-Canadian (see, for instance, Banting and Kymlicka 2004; Kazemipur 2006; Modood 2007). As well, in the specific case of Muslims, a few cross-national comparative studies of the assimilation experiences of immigrants in Europe and North America show that Canada is ahead of all other immigrant-receiving countries with regard to many indicators of successful integration (see, for instance, Vigdor 2011). A distinct history, a unique geography, and a special institutional profile are often cited as potential contributors to this "Canadian exceptionalism."

Given the notion of Canadian exceptionalism, a study of Muslim immigrants in a Canadian context is necessary for several reasons. First, the claim that things are different in Canada needs to be substantiated by more thorough studies. Second, if things are indeed different in Canada, we need to know what features of Canadian society have contributed to this difference. An inadequate or inaccurate understanding of the reasons behind the Canadian advantage would fail to provide clear targets for policy-making efforts to reinforce it. Third, even if the Canadian context is very different from that of Europe (or the United States, for that matter), improvements in communications technology mean that European and American concerns could migrate to Canada, generating similar responses to a problem that may not even exist. The great danger in a situation like this is that the responses given and the solutions adopted in one country have the potential to be viewed as universal and, therefore, to be uncritically adopted and implemented in other countries (which may have totally different histories and contexts). This is far from a remote possibility as the political discourses surrounding the Muslim question in various European countries and in the United States have already started to converge, despite enormous contextual differences (Cessari 2005).

Against this background, the focal point of *The Muslim Question in Canada* is an examination of the issue of Muslim exceptionalism in the context of Canadian exceptionalism. This is a timely and needed task as these phrases, with their respective connotations of uniqueness, could function to hinder further probing and could blind us to subtle changes in the situation. In a global environment filled with constant economic, technological, and cultural change, and with a high degree of population and capital mobility, the status quo is not static. This book is an attempt to determine (1) whether Canada is an exception with regard to the issue of Muslim immigrant integration and, thus, capable of serving as a model for the rest of the world; or (2) whether Muslim immigrant integration is a problem in Canada as well and, thus, in need of greater study.

In trying to address these issues, I have been guided by two fundamental considerations – one being more methodological in nature, the other more conceptual. Methodologically, I have been guided, for the most part, by empirical and triangulatory research. As much as possible, I have tried not to stop at the level of theory but, rather, to go beyond that to test competing hypotheses. This is a consequence of my dissatisfaction with the purely theoretical nature of a large portion of the existing work in this field of research. While very helpful with regard to suggesting theoretical possibilities, such contributions do little to tell us which of these are actually occurring on the ground. The studies that have attempted to add empirical data to theoretical discussions, on the other hand, have done so by using only one or another source or type of data. To mitigate this limitation, I use both qualitative and quantitative data from multiple sources while trying to incorporate as much empirical information as possible.

The conceptual considerations that guide this study are related to the theoretical framework used to examine the integration of immigrants. My reading of the literature has shown me that a better understanding of the nature and the future of the relationship between Muslim immigrants and host societies requires a shift in our conceptual framework, from one based on *culture* to one that takes into account the *structural* and *relational* dimensions at work. A culturalist approach gives too much weight to the influence of cultural orientations in shaping one's attitudes, behaviours, and position in society; it also treats those orientations as fixed. Not only does such an approach fail to explain the current state of affairs but it also presents the situation as unchangeable. A structuralist approach, however, adds more to the picture by taking into account economic, political, and social elements, hence offering a much richer understanding. For its part, given its premise that the current state of affairs is the outcome of a history of interaction between individuals and groups, a relational approach allows for flexibility and change.

Using the above theoretical premises, I break down the integration of immigrants – including Muslim immigrants – into the receiving societies as a multidimensional process involving four different domains: (1) the institutional, (2) the media, (3) the economic, and (4) the social. Depending on the nature of the relationship between the two groups in each of these four domains, one could expect to find either positive or negative, healthy or unhealthy, normal or problematic situations. As well, distinguishing these four domains allows us to locate the problematic areas more precisely, which, in turn, results in a more refined picture for further analysis, more sharply focused research, and more effective policy interventions.

At the risk of offering my conclusions prematurely, I would like to mention some of my general findings. First, the status of the relationship between Muslims and the rest of Canadian society is not as worrisome as seems to be the case in some Western European countries, such as France, the United Kingdom, Germany, and the Netherlands. That said, despite the relatively better status of Muslims in Canada, when Muslims are compared with other immigrants in the country they fall behind in many different areas. Also worrisome is the fact that Muslims have serious concerns about their future in Canada. Last, the major obstacles Muslims face in integrating into Canadian society lie not in the institutional or media domains but, rather, in the economic and social domains. This particular combination is found neither in the United States nor in Western Europe. It seems to be a uniquely Canadian situation and, therefore, the responses to it should also be place-specific.

General Approach

In conducting the research for this book, I was greatly influenced by the late French sociologist Pierre Bourdieu, and it is his approach to social phenomena that influences both the theoretical and methodological aspects of my work. Bourdieu's first influence on my work involves his disciplinary and theoretical eclecticism, reflected in what Loic Wacquant describes as his "utter disregard for disciplinary boundaries, the unusually broad spectrum of domains of specialized inquiry ... and its ability to blend a variety of sociological styles" (quoted in Webb, Schirato, and Danaher 2002). Such eclecticism is characteristic of mature problem-oriented research as, clearly, social problems do not recognize human-made boundaries. Just as physical reality consists of a tangle of chemical, physical, and biological components whose boundaries are impermeable, so social reality consists of a tangle of social, political, economic, and psychological components. To the extent that it is humanly possible, a researcher should be open to the possibility of moving across disciplinary boundaries and into non-comfort zones. I have tried to make this the foundation of my approach to Muslim integration and, in so doing, have, when required, left my home discipline (sociology) to delve into political science, economics, political philosophy, and social psychology.

A second Bourdieuian influence involves my use of a few of his key concepts, such as "field," "habitus," and "capital" (Bourdieu 2005). A detailed discussion of these concepts is provided in the following chapters, but it is necessary here to point out that, for Bourdieu, the use of these concepts provided a way out of the unhealthy debate between "structuralist" and "agency-based" theoretical camps within the social sciences. The former emphasizes the role of non-individual mega-forces (e.g., culture and structure) in shaping social developments, while the latter emphasizes human agency (for a thorough discussion of this debate, see Archer [1996, 2001]). In their most extreme versions, these two camps suggest, respectively, a purely deterministic view of social dynamics and a purely voluntaristic view. Bourdieu provides a way out of this dichotomy that is both flexible and explanatory.

Third, like Bourdieu, instead of adopting an atheoretical empiricist position or indulging in "pure" theorizing – which, in the words of Webb, Schirato, and Danaher (2002), is typical of the Anglo-American social sciences and the more philosophy-oriented fields like philosophy, literature, and cultural studies, respectively – I opt for a healthy dialogue between the two (for examples of this approach, see Bourdieu and Coleman [1991]). Bourdieu shows his great commitment to the dialogue between theory and empirical research in the preface of one of his first works, *Algeria 1960*:

> Regarding this text, written more than a decade ago, I more than once felt the wish to refine and systematize the analyses, by investing in them all that

subsequent work has yielded ... But, conscious of the futility of all forms of "theoretical labour" that are not accompanied by empirical work on the things themselves (which would mean, in this case, a return to fieldwork which is not possible at present), I have refrained from doing so. (Bourdieu 1979, viii)

Fourth, in trying to inform theoretical arguments through empirical research, I followed Bourdieu, who utilized a wide spectrum of data and data-gathering methods, "from painstaking ethnographic accounts to statistical models" (Wacquant, quoted in Webb, Schirato, and Danaher 2002). Examples of this approach may be found in many of Bourdieu's works (e.g., Bourdieu 2005). Bourdieu (1993) describes his approach as deliberate and as based on the fact that ethnographic observations and statistical analyses have two entirely different goals. This is because the former "can only be based on a small number of cases" while the latter allows the researcher to "establish regularities and to situate the observed cases in the universe of the existing cases." He adds that "the analyses that are described as 'qualitative' are ... essential for understanding, that is to say fully explaining, what the statistics merely record" (14).

While Bourdieu's methodological heterodoxy was not shared by many social scientists of his time (who were still trapped in their methodological paradigms), its popularity is now on the rise and, since the mid-1990s, has been embodied in the newly emerging methodological approach known as "mixed methods" (Creswell 2006; Johnson and Onwuegbuzie 2004; Teddlie and Tashakkori 2009). The philosophical foundation of the mixed methods approach to social issues is pragmatism, which, according to Teddlie and Tashakkori (2009, 7), involves "advocating the use of whatever methodological tools are required to answer the research questions under study." In utilizing a mixed methods approach, "investigators go back and forth seamlessly between statistical and thematic analysis" (8). In my work, the reader will find many examples of this movement between qualitative and quantitative data. With some exceptions, my research basically involves using (1) quantitative methods to detect general patterns and anomalies and (2) qualitative methods to develop hypotheses and theoretical possibilities. The latter two are then used to make sense of the former two.

At the heart of the above exercise is a notion that Bourdieu uses widely but discusses only briefly – that is, comparative method (see, for instance, Bourdieu 1984). Initially, comparative method was viewed as an antidote to statistical method. For example, in response to Smelser's argument regarding the inferiority of comparative method to statistical method, Ragin (1987) argues that the former is superior to the latter for four different reasons. First, "the statistical method is not combinatorial," meaning that it treats each independent variable separately, even when controlling for the impacts of other relevant variables. In other words, statistical method cannot effectively address the impact of the combination of independent variables. He acknowledges that this can be done through adding interaction effects to the analysis but finds the sheer number of such effects to be incorporated prohibitive. Second, comparative method pays closer attention to irregularities and outlier cases (as opposed to statistical method, which focuses on regularities and general patterns), and this is particularly useful "for the task of building new theories and synthesizing existing theories" (16). Third, "the comparative method does not require the investigator to pretend that he or she has a sample of societies drawn from a particular population so that tests of statistical significance can be used." And, finally, "the comparative method forces the investigator to become familiar with the cases relevant to the analysis" and to "examine each case directly and compare each case with all other relevant cases" (ibid.). According to Ragin, the difference between comparative method and statistical method is that the former is case-oriented while the latter is variable-oriented. However, combined strategies also exist, and they fall into one of two camps: "Examples of combined strategies include variable-oriented analyses supplemented with case studies ... and case studies reinforced with quantitative analyses" (17).

The problem with comparative method, particularly when used by qualitative scholars, is that, while it helps with theory building, it does not allow for theory testing. So, in a sense, this method is more an extension of theory than a research method per se. Ragin (1987, 11) himself acknowledges this when he says: "but many comparativists, especially those who are qualitatively oriented, are not often involved in 'testing' theories per se. Rather, they *apply* theory to cases in order to interpret them." I combine comparative and statistical approaches by using variable-oriented quantitative work to find general patterns and to test theories, while using comparative qualitative methods to develop insights, theories, and hypotheses, to interpret quantitative findings, and to make sense of anomalies.

The general points that inform my conceptual framework and methodological strategy are as follows:

1 I use a disciplinary and theoretical eclecticism, drawing on the relevant findings and propositions of scholars in various academic fields and of different theoretical persuasions.
2 I apply an integrated theoretical-empirical approach, in which every effort is made to empirically test and verify the theoretical hypotheses. Also, when theories are unable to explain the observed trends, I attempt to formulate an alternative theory or to suggest modifications to the initial propositions.
2 I employ a combined quantitative-qualitative research method, using various sources of data and types of analysis, from the statistical analysis of survey data, through the analysis of face-to-face interview data, to participant observation. With occasional variations, I use the qualitative data to develop conceptual understandings and hypotheses (i.e., theory building) as well as to analyze and interpret the quantitative findings. I use quantitative data to detect trends and anomalies as well as to test theories.
4 To the extent that it is possible and useful, I use a comparative approach to put things in perspective. I do this by drawing comparisons between various groups (e.g., between immigrants and the native-born, and between genders, religions, and national origins within immigrant groups).

Outline of the Book

The Muslim Question in Canada is divided into four parts. Part 1 deals with the big picture – that is, the broad outlines of the issue of the Muslim question and the existing perspectives on this issue. Chapter 2 reviews the socio-demographic aspects of the encounter between Muslims and Western liberal democracies, while Chapter 3 reviews how the Muslim question has been understood and addressed. I provide examples of each of the main perspectives and review their strengths and weaknesses.

Part 2 includes Chapters 4 and 5, which discuss the conceptual framework that I propose for studying not only the Muslim question but also the more general issue of the integration of immigrants into host societies. This framework has been influenced primarily by the sociologists Pierre Bourdieu and Charles Tilly, the Nobel-Laureate-economist-turned-political-philosopher Amartya Sen, and the various "contact theory" scholars in the field of social psychology. Its overarching assumption is that the nature of the integration of (Muslim) immigrants into their new countries depends on the quality of the interaction between them and the host society, including the latter's institutional, media, economic, and social domains.

The chapters included in Part 3 examine various aspects of the lives of Muslims in Canada. The goal of these chapters is to determine the extent to which the Canadian situation is similar to or different from those in Europe and the United States. Chapter 6 looks at the qualitative discussions on this issue, while Chapter 7 looks at the quantitative data. The findings reported in this section show that the Muslim question is not as severe in Canada as it is in some other countries, but they also indicate that there are areas in need of particular attention.

Part 4 includes four chapters that dig deeper into the factors behind the patterns found and reported in Part 3. Chapter 8 examines the economic factors while Chapter 9 addresses the social. Chapter 10 offers some suggestions regarding the kind of measures that could improve the status of Muslims in Canada, while Chapter 11, the last chapter, discusses the implications of this study. These implications are discussed under two headings: (1) those concerned with immigrant settlement policies and practices, and (2) those concerned with theoretical issues in debates about multiculturalism. Chapter 11 also attempts to offer some general ideas about possible future paths for the relationships between Muslims and native-born Canadians. It concludes with a brief list of areas that need to be addressed in future research.

The content of each chapter is based on a variety of data sources, both qualitative and quantitative. The qualitative data are taken from a series of face-to-face interviews conducted with Muslim immigrants between 2009 and 2011. The twelve interviewees – all in their twenties and thirties – were selected through snowball sampling in the Prairie provinces, and efforts were made to maximize the diversity of the cases with regard to gender, national origin, and Islamic sect. The purpose of this component of the study is to gain insight into the situation of Muslim immigrants and to develop hypotheses that, later, would be examined through the use of quantitative methods. Some individuals were interviewed at a later time in order to help make sense of the quantitative findings.

The quantitative data come from the extensive nationwide surveys conducted by Statistics Canada, including the General Social Surveys (GSS), the Ethnic Diversity Survey (EDS), the Longitudinal Survey of Immigrants to Canada (LSIC), and the Canadian Census. In addition, I used two simultaneous surveys of Canadian Muslims and non-Muslims conducted by Environics in 2006. The first of these two surveys had a sample of five hundred Canadian Muslims, and the second had a sample of twenty-five hundred non-Muslim Canadians.

PART 1

CONTEXT

2
Muslims and/in the West

Muslims and the West: A Complex Encounter

For many ordinary consumers of media products the "Muslim question" – that is, the uneasy relationship between Muslims and others in Western countries – is simply a matter of cultural differences between the two groups. According to this view, the fault line lies between two sets of preferences, lifestyles, worldviews – one prone to an illiberal, violent, and non-compromising way of being, the other to a democratic, liberal, and tolerant way of being. The problems with such a binary picture are numerous; however, at their heart lie the two fallacies of reductionism and essentialism. Reductionism refers to attributing multifaceted and complex problems to one factor – here, culture or religion. Essentialism refers to the assumption that all those who belong to the same faith – Muslims, in this case – possess permanent and distinct attributes that guide their behaviours throughout their lives. By situating the Muslim question within this binary and culture-based framework, we ignore both geography and history – that is, we ignore the enormous diversity of attitudes and practices within the Muslim world and the complex and multi-stranded nature of the history of Islam. In other words, the culturally based perception of the Muslim question endows it with a false universality.

Recently, though, some attempts have been made to add a geographic and/or a historic dimension to the above argument. The most influential of these attempts are those put forward by Samuel Huntington and Bernard

Lewis. Huntington (1996), in *The Clash of Civilizations*, expands the geo-graphical scope of the Muslim question by placing it within a much broader and more global context (see Chapter 1). Bernard Lewis, on the other hand, points to history to find the origin of the conflictual relationship between Muslims and Westerners. In a book entitled *What Went Wrong?*, which was published shortly after the events of 9/11, Lewis (2002) attributes anti-Western sentiments in the Muslim world to a "blame game" on the part of Muslims – particularly those in the Middle East – who are attempting to deal with the rapid decline of Islamic civilization in the modern era. He considers this blame game to have been present throughout Muslim history but with its focus being on different groups at different times: Mongols for the Persians, Turks for the Arabs, Arabs for the Turks, British and French colonialism for all. In the most recent twist of this long history of the blame game, Lewis argues, the needle is now pointing to Westerners in general and to Americans and Jews in particular, not only as political opponents but also as proponents of secular lifestyles. In other words, the anger of Muslims towards non-Muslims is fed by the historical humiliation felt by the former and the roles they attribute to the latter. Despite their sophisticated nature, both Huntington's and Lewis's views remain culturalist at heart, with one trying to expand the scope of the Muslim question to a much bigger geo-graphic area and the other to a much longer historical time frame.

More nuanced accounts of the issue, however, are increasingly emer-ging, and the picture is becoming more crowded through the addition of new elements, such as the changing global religious landscape and the role played by religion in various nation-building projects. Cliteur (2010), for instance, argues that, within the last two decades of the twentieth century, the global religious landscape has gone through some radical transformations, with implications for the Muslim question. During this period, according to Cliteur, while Christianity grew modestly, Islam grew exponentially, as did atheism. This demographic shift changed the appear-ance of some old debates involving religion – for example, faith versus rea-son, religion versus state – by giving Islam a much more visible place. Not only that, the intensity of these debates also shifted to a higher gear, given the claim of Islamic teachings regarding the regulation of the mundane sphere of life on top of the conventional Christian claim regarding the regu-lation of the spiritual sphere of life. Unlike the rivalry between Christianity and atheism, which was over two separate spheres of life (the spiritual and the mundane), the rivalry between secular forces and Islam would be over the same sphere – the so-called "this-worldly" sphere.

A different source of tension between Muslims and Westerners is suggested by Hurd (2008), and this involves the role played by Islam in the process of nation building in the West. She argues that, historically, the national identity of Americans as well as of Europeans (as members of nations run by secular democracies) were shaped in response and reaction to Islam. In this perspective, the notion of secular democracy finds its most articulate expression in contradistinction to a highly religious and undemocratic Muslim world. In other words, regardless of what might have happened throughout history, Muslims served as the "other" against which the West established its secular democratic features.

This is not an experience unique to Muslims. Anthony Marx (2003), for instance, points to the formation of the French national identity in reaction to Protestantism, and that of the British in response to Roman Catholicism. Historically, such processes were often triggered when something managed to undermine a country's shared national identity. As soon as it appears as though an "us-versus-them" dichotomy will be useful, people start looking for a group that can be transformed into a "them," against which a "we" can shape itself. Sometimes this other is another country; but, more frequently, it is comprised of religious minorities within the same country (this being a less costly alternative).

The "Jewish question" was the product of a similar nation-building project in late-nineteenth-century Europe, with Jews supplying the needed "other" (GhaneaBassiri 2010). One could argue that, under the pressures of globalization, regionalization, and extreme individualization, many countries in the West feel a need to create an other against which to unite.

Hurd (2008) makes a second point with direct implications for the Muslim question. She argues that the current formulations of secularism – that is, the notion of the separation of religion and state – carries the implicit assumption that such a separation is possible either only when religion is abandoned (as in the *laicite* variation of secularism dominant in Europe and particularly in France) or only within the confines of the Judeo-Christian faith (as in the version of secularism dominant in North America). It is also assumed that Muslims are not prone to secularism in either of these two scenarios, partly due to their strong attachment to their faith but also due to the particular nature of their religion, which does not allow for an easy separation between the spiritual and the mundane. A logical extension of this argument is that, given Muslims' difficulties with the notion of secularism, the Muslim immigrant will find it difficult to live within secular Western democracies.

If nothing else, the above accounts show that the problem at hand is certainly far too complicated and multilayered to be explained by simplistic univariate theories. In fact, there are several complicating factors that need to be taken into consideration before issuing universal statements. One such factor is that, in the uneasy relationship between Muslims and the West, neither of the two sides is a monolithic entity. The history of Islam shows that, underneath the umbrella category of Islam, there are at least three identifiable variations – Arab, Turkish, and Persian – each of which consists of localized and domesticized versions combining common Islamic principles and local and regional traditions. One could argue that, in its encounter with Islam, the West could be separated into three different regions: southwestern Europe, east-central Europe, and North America. Before moving forward, we should take a look at these diverse entities.

Not only are the three variations of Islam very different from each other but they have also experienced tensions among themselves and, at times, bloody conflicts. The better-known part of this history is related to the distinction between the Persian part of the Muslim world, which belongs to the Shia branch of Islam (with some smaller Shia pockets outside Iran) and the rest of the Muslim world, which is predominantly Sunni. These two branches of Islam originally differed on their views about who should succeed Prophet Muhammad; later, they came to have very distinct theologies, rituals, and articles of faith. As time passed, such historical distinctions created a fault line in the Muslim Middle East, with the Arab Sunni Muslims on one side and the Persian/Iranian Shia Muslims on the other.

Both of these branches of Islam came into conflict with the Turkish branch during the era of the Ottoman Empire. Having captured most of the Arab Muslim world in the Middle East and North Africa, the Ottomans ruled these areas for nearly five centuries, only to be fended off through a coalition of Arab and Western European forces. On their southeastern border, during the *Safavid* dynasty (sixteenth to eighteenth centuries) and *Qajar* dynasty (mid-eighteenth to early-twentieth centuries), the Ottomans were in an almost constant state of conflict with the Shia Persians. Even in today's Muslim world, one can easily see the presence of these three major historical players – Arab, Persian, and Turkish – competing for the hearts and souls of Muslims as well as for the upper hand in Muslim affairs. Most recently, the Middle East has become the stage for a fierce competition between three different models of "Islamic governance": the Iranian-style Islamic republic, the Saudi-style Islamic kingdom, and the Turkish-style Islamic democracy.

Besides this enormous diversity regarding the ways in which the various Muslim countries arrived at Islam, there is also a fair bit of diversity regarding the ways in which Western countries came into contact with the Muslim world. Interestingly, each of the three parts of the Western world – southwestern Europe, east-central Europe, and North America – came into contact predominantly and respectively with one of the components of the Muslim world. As Lewis (1987) argues, the initial contacts between Islam and Europe were a result of the expansionist policies of the Islamic Caliphate, which brought the Arab Muslims of the Middle East and North Africa to the southwestern corner of Europe (Spain, Italy, France). The counterattacks by Christian Europe, through the eleventh-century crusades, eventually succeeded in pushing Muslims back and, in the process, brought Europeans to Syria and Palestine. Here, the Crusaders "encountered the new champions of Islam – the Turks – who by now governed most of the Middle East ... [T]he Turks and their associates held and eventually threw back the Christian invaders and began a new advance which once again brought Islam into Europe – this time at the eastern end and in a Turkish form" (xiv-xv). From this, it is easy to infer that the understanding of Islam and Muslims among the east-central Europeans (such as the Austrians) revolved mostly around the Turkish variation, while that of the southwestern European countries revolved mostly around the Arabs. The Persian variation of Islam did not become a part of this portrayal of Muslims until the late twentieth century, when the ongoing encounter between Iran and the United States (in the course of Iran's Islamic Revolution and its aftermath) began. From this picture, it is apparent that, historically, Islam presented itself in its Arab variation to southwestern Europeans, in its Turkish variation to east-central Europeans, and in its Persian variation to North Americans. Hence, in the debates about Islam and Muslims taking place in the West, each party's understanding of Muslims' attitudes and lifestyles is influenced by its specific historical experiences.

This historical diversity in the encounters between Islam and the West aside, the interactions between Muslim minorities and non-Muslim majorities within many Western countries today continue to show a great deal of variation. For one thing, Muslims currently living in various European countries are much less diverse than those living in North America. For example, Muslims in France come predominantly from North Africa; those in Britain from South Asia (India, Pakistan, and Bangladesh); and those in Germany from Turkey (for a good survey of the sources and historical experiences of Muslims in European countries, see Hunter 2002). This pattern, in most cases, reflects past colonial ties – ties that do not exist for non-European countries. Moreover, the United States is the only country that has, besides its immigrant Muslim population, a significant local Muslim population – the African-American Muslims – with a much longer history and very distinct set of concerns, priorities, and outlooks. In Canada, neither of these two features – colonial ties or a local Muslim population – is present, and this means that Muslims in this country tend to be ethnically diverse as well as overwhelmingly immigrant.

With all this in mind, it is now time to look at the general profile of the Canadian Muslim population and to consider some of its unique features. An awareness of these features is crucial to a better understanding of the status of Muslims in this country and of the dynamics of their relationship with the broader population.

Muslims in Canada: A Distinct Encounter

Canada's encounter with Muslims is unlike that of any of the other major immigrant-receiving countries. It has a very short history with no colonial past, and Canada has a Muslim population that is both diverse and carefully selected. These unique features reinforce the expectation that the experiences of Muslims in Canada may be quite different from those of Muslims in other immigrant-receiving countries.

The historical accounts of Muslims' presence in Canada cite the 1850s or 1870s as the time when the first Muslims came to this country, and the 1930s as the time when the first mosque was established. None of these accounts, however, indicates a sizable Muslim presence. Up to the early years of the twentieth century, most of the Muslims living in Canada were of Croatian origin, with some coming from territories under Ottoman rule – notably Turkey and Syria (Zine 2008). According to Abu-Laban, with the outbreak of the First World War, Canadian authorities viewed Turkish Muslim immigrants as enemy aliens and started to send them back to their country of origin; as a result, until after the Second World War, the population of Canadian Muslims remained relatively small (cited in Zine 2008, 5). It was only in the early 1970s that Muslims started arriving in large numbers, and this was thanks to the late-1960s reforms to Canadian immigration laws, which replaced the quotas on immigration from Asia and Africa and the discretionary powers of immigration officials who used "criteria emphasizing education, skills and the employability of the applicant" (Hamdani 1999, 203).

While the increase in the population of Canadian Muslims is obvious, an accurate count of that population is difficult to attain, largely due to the way in which the Canadian census is structured. In contrast to countries such as Australia, where the population has to complete only one census questionnaire, which includes a question on religious background, Canadian census data are gathered through two questionnaires, only one of which asks about the respondents' religious background – and that particular questionnaire is administered to only 20 percent of the population. Thus, total counts of faith communities are estimated by extrapolating information from one-fifth of the population and extending it to the entire population. This means that any count of the population of various religions in Canada, including Muslims, is, at best, an estimate.

There are three additional wrinkles to how we attempt to acquire an accurate estimate of the population of Muslims in Canada. First, the question on religion in the "long-form" census is administered only in every other census (e.g., 1981, 1991, 2001, and 2011). Second, starting with the 2011 census, filling out the long-form was declared optional. As a result, those randomly selected to fill in the questionnaire are no longer under any pressure to do so, with the result that there is no guarantee that the returned questionnaires accurately reflect the intended and initial sampling design. This means that the 2001 census offers the last reasonably reliable data available for the purpose of estimating the population of faith groups. In the case of Muslims, an additional problem is that, in 1941, the category "Muslim" was dropped from the Canadian census questionnaire, only to be reintroduced forty years later (Hamdani 1999, 198). This has resulted in a significant gap in the official information on the Muslim population in Canada in the post-Second World War period. However, the fact that the population of Muslims in Canada started to rise only since the early 1970s makes this information gap less serious than it might have been.

The absence of a reliable estimate of the population of Canadian Muslims has resulted in different parties attempting to provide estimates, with differing results. Hamdani (1999) extensively documents these attempts and their unreliability. Many of them were clearly influenced by political agendas, such as giving an inflated estimate of the Muslim population either to claim a bigger share of whatever resources were there or to create a fear of Muslims. The unreliability of these estimates is evident in the figures suggested, which vary from between less than .25 million to higher than 1 million. By the mid-1990s, however, according to Hamdani, estimates started to converge towards more realistic and believable figures.

Those figures estimate the population of Muslims in Canada to be about 579,640 in 2001 (Statistics Canada 2001) and 940,000 in 2011 (Pew Research Center 2011). According to one estimate, the population of Canadian Muslims is expected to reach about 2 million in 2021 and slightly less than 3 million in 2031 (Mata 2011). If these predictions are proven to be accurate, they would imply that the population of Muslims, currently about 2.8 percent of the total population of Canada, will rise to about 6.6 percent by the year 2030 (Pew Research Center 2011). In that case, the proportion of Muslims in the total population of Canada at that time will be about four times that of its southern neighbour. This would be a significant jump in a relatively short period, meaning that Muslims would replace Jews as the largest religious minority in Canada (Hamdani 1999). This is an important fact to keep in mind when examining the relationship between Muslims and non-Muslims in Canada.

The rapid increase in the population of Canadian Muslims is due to two factors, the first of which is the arrival of a larger number of Muslim immigrants. The increase in the number of Muslim immigrants, as Figure 2.1 indicates, has raised the proportion of Muslims within the total immigrant population in Canada from around 2 percent in 1970 to around 20 percent in 2000. In addition to immigration, Muslims have a higher fertility rate than the host population. This higher rate is a product of the fact that Muslims are mostly first-generation immigrants, with many of them being in their child-bearing years. According to Hamdani (1999, 205), "Muslims are experiencing a baby-boom while the country as a whole is faced with low birth rates." While the momentum of this so-called Muslim baby-boom cohort will generate a higher birth rate among Muslims for quite some time, with the increase in the proportional size of second-generation Muslims, the fertility rates are likely to decline.

The awareness of a Muslim presence is not equally felt by all native-born Canadians as the population of Muslims is very unevenly distributed across the country. According to the most recent estimates by Statistics Canada (2005), 61 percent of all Canadian Muslims live in the nation's largest province, Ontario; 19 percent live in Quebec; and British Columbia and Alberta are almost tied for third place, with each hosting about 10 percent of the Canadian Muslim population. Like all basic demographic features, this uneven distribution of the population of Muslims has great implications for the types of experiences they have and the challenges they face. This is evident in the heavy debates that occurred during the past decade around the issues of "Sharia law" in Ontario, "reasonable accommodation" in Quebec,

FIGURE 2.1

Muslim immigrants as a percentage of total immigrants to Canada, by year of arrival

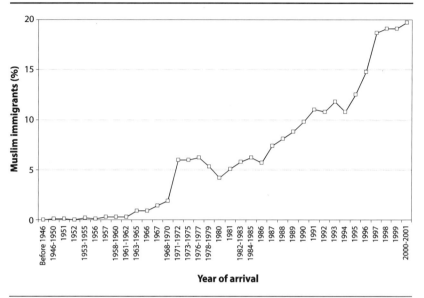

Source: Statistics Canada, Canadian Census, 2001.

and the recent election of the first Muslim mayor in Calgary, while the rest of the country has been relatively silent on the issue of Muslims in Canada.

The potential social and political implications of the preceding demographic facts are fourfold. First, the higher proportion of Muslims in the general Canadian population compared to, say, that in the general American population, could give Muslims more visibility in the eyes of native-born Canadians than in the eyes of native-born Americans. This could provide native-born Canadians with more opportunities to interact with Muslims as well as create more sensitivity among the host population. Second, a fast increase in the Muslim population could create a fear of extinction among the native-born population. Recently, several campaigns have been organized over the internet, their main thrust being to warn native-born Christians in Western countries that Muslims are a threat to take over their population in the near future. Such campaigns often call for a halt to immigration from Muslim countries. One would expect that such campaigns would have the strongest impact in regions in which they align with people's observations of demographic changes on the streets.

Third, the greater diversity of the Muslim population in Canada, as compared to other Western countries, creates a totally different dynamic both within the Muslim community and in its relationship with the broader society. Among Muslims, this diversity leads to an increased level of interaction between Muslims of various national, cultural, and linguistic backgrounds. However, when it comes to the interaction between Muslims and non-Muslims, such diversity might cause problems as it could make the task of learning about Muslims much more demanding for non-Muslims. The enormity of this task could then result in a withdrawal from interaction.

Finally, the uneven distribution of the Muslim population in different regions and cities within Canada can result in the increased visibility of Muslims in some areas but not others. The heavy concentration in some areas could create tensions and conflicts, which could then easily travel to other regions through mass media. The debates and images that travel in this way could, in turn, negatively influence the native-born population in those areas with a less visible Muslim presence. This dynamic is already happening with regard to Europe and the rest of the Western world: the severe tensions between Muslims and the local populations in countries such as France and the Netherlands have generated debates that have crossed borders and spread into countries with totally different social environments.

Having seen the large context within which the Muslim question should be studied as well as the complex, multilayered nature of encounters between Muslims and the Western world, it is now time to review the various attempts to address this question.

3

Responses to the Muslim Question

Due to the recent emergence of what is termed the "Muslim question," there have been very few responses to it. Most are of a broad nature, addressing the general issues of ethnic/cultural diversity of populations, relationships between majority-minority groups, and integration of immigrants into host societies – with occasional references to Muslim minorities and/or immigrants. As discussed in Chapter 1, however, a great deal of the recent debate and discussion surrounding these issues has, explicitly or implicitly, revolved around Muslims. The most popular explanations for Muslims' perceived slow integration into host societies hold that they are either unwilling or unable to do so. Such accounts reveal a basic assumption: the belief that the factors influencing Muslims' attitudes and behaviours are drastically different from those influencing those of people of other religious and cultural backgrounds, particularly those living in Western democracies. This results in the notion of "Muslim exceptionalism."

Traces of the notion of Muslim exceptionalism as an explanation for issues involving Muslims can be found in several different debates. The oldest and probably the best known is manifested in the body of literary and non-literary works that Edward Said (1979) refers to as "Orientalism." The essence of Orientalism, according to Said, is a perceived fundamental distinction between the West (Occident) and the East (Orient), as found mostly in the works of French and British academic and literary figures over the past couple of centuries. The same idea was later used by others as an explanation for the absence of economic development in the contemporary Muslim world, the antagonism between Muslims and the West, the lack of political democracies in Muslim countries (see Hashemi 2009), the slow growth of secularism in Muslim societies and, last and most relevant to my study, the unwillingness and/or inability of Muslims to live in secular democracies and to play by democratic rules.

This perceived unwillingness and/or inability of Muslims to live peacefully in secular democracies is tied to a set of perceptions about Muslims: for example, their strong attachment to their faith, the illiberal contents of their religion, the "all-encompassing" nature of Islam (i.e., it covers both private and public domains), their proclivity for violence, the predominance of tribal-like loyalties among Muslims, and so on. Such perceptions heavily inform the debates involving Muslims and, from time to time, result in the advocacy of harsh and extreme measures, such as the need to halt immigration from Muslim countries altogether (e.g., Fox News 2012, panel discussion) and to deport millions of Muslim immigrants living in the West (e.g., Wilders 2011). Such extremist views rest on the assumption that the source of the problem is in the Muslim mindset.

Such extremist views, however, inform only one of many approaches to the issue of minority-majority relations in general and to that of Muslim immigrants-host country in particular. There are numerous solutions to these issues, and these vary according to whether they emphasize the cultural, the political, or the economic as well as according to who should be the main agent of change – the minority, the majority, or both. Below, I first classify these various views and then proceed to discuss their main shortcomings. Later (Chapter 4), I suggest an alternative approach to understanding and addressing the Muslim question.

There are at least three ways to classify existing accounts, responses, and policies regarding the integration of minorities and immigrants in general and Muslims in particular. The first type of classification concerns the target agency. In other words, *who* is supposed to take the initiative for integration: minorities (immigrants, Muslims), the majority, or both. The second type of classification concerns the domain in which such initiatives should be taken and the nature of the activities in question. In other words, *what* is supposed to be done for integration to happen? What cultural, political, or economic changes are needed? The third type of classification concerns *where* integration has to happen and where its signs might be found: in behaviours, in information, or in emotions (symbolically, these may be viewed as related to body, mind, and soul, respectively). The classifications who, what, and where are not mutually exclusive, and each response to the issue of diversity could be placed within all three. Below, I provide a more detailed description of these various classifications, along with examples of each.

Classification of Perspectives on Integration: Who, What, and Where

As far as the agent of integration – the *who* question – is concerned, the oldest and most deep-seated response sees integration primarily as the responsibility of minorities. The reasoning behind this line of thinking is that the baseline is the majority and, especially in democratic societies, the majority sets the rules and standards by which the minority should abide. The theory of assimilation is a prime example of this approach. In its most classic version, the notion of assimilation concerns the cultural orientation of immigrants and minorities, but the same spirit resides in more recent versions, in which assimilation is expected to include participating in the political and civic life of the host societies, subscribing to the majority's work ethic, and taking responsibility for one's economic life without relying on the financial support of the host government.

Another view on who should be responsible for integration focuses on the majority. In this primarily liberal view, the minority has a right to keep its cultural heritage and the majority is expected to educate itself about minority cultures. This view results in the inclusion of materials on minority cultures in school curricula (e.g., Aboriginal peoples in Canada, African Americans in the United States) and in anti-racism education. It has cultural education at its heart, but it also has a more political variation, in which the emphasis is not only on the right of minorities to keep their own cultures but also on the responsibility of majority institutions to develop policies that "recognize" this right and actively promote it. An economic variation of this view puts more emphasis on anti-discrimination policies and awareness in such environments as the job market.

Another view regarding who should be responsible for integration involves both majority and minority populations. While this view, like the other two, remains primarily cultural in orientation, it is distinct from them in that it emphasizes a need for better understanding on both sides. A lot of recent "*inter*-cultural" dialogues and "*inter*-faith" initiatives are primarily informed by such a view.

The question of *where* integration should take place – in one's behaviours (body), brain (mind), or heart (soul) – adds another layer to the issue of integration. For a lot of people, integration is primarily seen as a matter of the members of the minority abiding by certain behavioural expectations, such as obeying the law, following the host society's dress code, keeping neighbourhoods clean, speaking the language of the host society in public spaces (perhaps even at home), working for their living, voting in elections, participating in volunteer activities, and participating in national celebrations. From this perspective, which focuses on the body, the signs of integration are clearly visible.

Those who focus on the mind are basically concerned about the need for immigrants and minorities to learn the language, history, and culture of the host society as well as its political system and the names of people in power. It is this kind of approach to integration that results in the emphasis on things such as writing citizenship exams and taking language courses. While all these certainly add to the level of comfort that a minority has with regard to the majority and vice versa, they do not touch on the true measure of integration – emotional attachment (i.e., attachment at the level of the soul).

Emotional attachment to a country may certainly manifest itself through how one behaves (body) or what one knows (mind), but the existence of the latter two does not guarantee the existence of the former. Emotional attachment to a country is likely to be associated with one's sense of belonging to that country, the development of a shared sense of national identity, satisfaction with the decision to migrate, happiness with one's post-migration experiences, and a desire to stay in one's new country permanently. In the absence of this emotional attachment, neither of the two other dimensions of integration can ensure that one remains a faithful member of one's newly adopted country. Depending on who and what is emphasized, the various responses to the integration question fall into one or more of the following three categories of attachment: behavioural (body), intellectual (mind), and emotional (soul).

With the above points in mind, we can use Table 3.1 to classify the existing perspectives on integration on the basis of *who* should take the initiative, *what* needs to be done, and *where* the main changes are expected to occur. Cell 1, the cultural education approach, is something to be practised by majority institutions (like schools, workplaces, etc.) with the purpose of creating awareness among the majority regarding the cultural traits of minorities. Cell 2, the politics of recognition approach, similarly addresses the host society's institutions, expecting those institutions to provide a space for minorities to retain and promote their cultural heritages. Through such activities, minorities will be able to develop their genuine identities free from the impositions of the majority culture/identity; hence, an awareness of their cultural heritage and a sense of pride in it, which touches both their minds and their souls. Along the same line, Cell 3 represents the anti-discrimination approach as the responsibility of the majority population and public institutions. Cell 4, representing the old assimilationist view, holds that minorities, and particularly immigrants, have a responsibility to convert to the culture of the majority by virtue of their decision to voluntarily emigrate from their countries of origin. It follows that, if immigrants are uncomfortable with such a conversion, they should either return to their countries of origin or accept the risk of living an isolated life in the host society, deprived of some of the basic rights enjoyed by other citizens. The essence of assimilation revolves around the conversion of ways of thinking (mind) and styles of behaving (body).

Cell 5 is promoted primarily by minority advocates who would like to see immigrants engage more extensively in the political process of their new homes, both to show their attachment to the country and to influence the decisions affecting their lives. This involves active participation in civic and political processes, which is clearly a behavioural development (body). Cell 6 represents the view of those who think the backlash against immigrants and diversity is, at least partly, driven by their over-reliance on public transfers and social programs such as employment insurance, disability services, pension payments, and welfare support. The suggestion is that immigrants should subscribe to an outlook that emphasizes hard work and individual economic responsibility. Cell 7 shows a more recent development in the field – inter-cultural and/or infer-faith dialogue – influenced by the belief that a great number of problems in inter-group relations are rooted in cultural misunderstandings and that those misunderstandings may be alleviated by learning more about each other's cultures. The underlying assumption is that, through these efforts, it will become obvious to both the majority and the minority that they have much more in common than they had initially imagined.

Of these seven scenarios and approaches, Cells 1 and 4 come about mostly in response to general diversity issues and are not necessarily associated with Muslims; they mostly refer either to national minorities (such as African Americans in the United States or Aboriginal peoples in Canada) or to pre-1960s immigrants (who came to North America largely from Europe). Cells 2, 5, and 7, however, are more heavily associated with Muslims. True, Cell 2, the politics of recognition, does not contain any particular reference

TABLE 3.1

Classification of perspectives on integration: Who, what, and where

| | | *WHAT (nature of the problem/solution)* | | |
		Cultural	Political	Economic
WHO (agent of change)	Majority	❶ Cultural education/ anti-racism (*WHERE:* Mind)	❷ Politics of recognition (*WHERE:* Mind-Soul)	❸ Anti-discrimination (*WHERE:* Body)
	Minority	❹ Assimilation/ exclusion (*WHERE:* Body/Mind)	❺ Political engagement (*WHERE:* Body)	❻ No welfare- dependency (*WHERE:* Body)
	Majority and minority	❼ Inter-faith dialogue (*WHERE:* Mind)		

to Muslim minorities, but this approach became popular and informed multiculturalism policies at the time that the integration of Muslim immigrants became an issue; consequently, the debates around this soon took on a heavy Muslim twist. The inter-faith dialogues (Cell 7) were around before, but their popularity rose after 9/11, and this time they frequently included Muslims. Cell 5, the encouragement of immigrant minorities to practise political engagement, was also around and was practised by other immigrants, but a particular version of it was developed by moderate Muslim leaders and scholars living in primarily non-Muslim countries. These people were specifically concerned with addressing the challenges faced by Muslims and the possible benefits of their increased engagement in the social and political life of their host countries. Below, I introduce some of the most articulate and influential examples of the ideas, policies, and initiatives informed by the perspectives presented in Table 3.1. These ideas have been proposed by a variety of thinkers, governments, and organizations in response to specific circumstances, but some of them have managed to transcend these circumstances to provide general perspectives on the issue of diversity. These include Cells 2, 4, and 5, which I discuss below.

Assimilation/Exclusion (Cell 4)

Until the early 1990s, assimilation theory was the dominant mode of understanding the experiences of immigrants in host societies, and, consequently, it shaped and informed the bulk of immigration research. After falling out of favour for a while, a decade later the assimilationist perspective seems to be making a comeback. In its first life, assimilation was used mainly to describe what immigrants typically do after migration; in its recent incarnation, it is used mainly to prescribe what immigrants *should* do after migration.

The premise of assimilationist theory is straightforward: the longer they stay in the host countries, the more immigrants manage to diminish language and cultural barriers, enter into social relationships with the host population, get more education in the host country, improve their occupational skills, enter into job-finding networks or build up their own, and, as a result, start their upward mobility. On the economic front, it is argued that, although immigrants' earnings are lower than those of non-immigrants at the time of arrival, they tend to equalize within ten to fifteen years and then surpass them, partly due to immigrants' being highly motivated, ambitious, and ready to work longer and harder than non-immigrants (Carliner 1980). Second-generation immigrants are believed to follow this path at an even faster pace because they do not have to face some of the hardships that their parents faced, such as language barriers and the recognition of educational credentials. In other words, assimilationist theory implies that the socioeconomic status of immigrants correlates positively with the length of time in their host country and negatively with their age at arrival. The process of immigrants' integration into host societies is viewed, in this perspective, not only as straightforward and successful but also as inevitable.

The experiences of most recent immigrants – mostly those arriving in the last two decades of the twentieth century and emigrating from non-European sources – posed serious challenges to the validity, or at least the universality, of the assimilation process. These new immigrants did not seem to sail smoothly through the economic, social, and cultural oceans of their host societies. In trying to explain the difficulty of the economic integration of immigrants, some individuals, like the prominent American immigration researcher George Borjas (1994, 1713), point out that "the costs and benefits of immigration were radically altered during the 1980s, and a number of new questions, issues, and perceptions replaced them." For example: "[The] relative skills of successive immigrant waves declined over much of the postwar period; it is unlikely that recent immigrants will reach parity with the earnings of natives during their working lives; ... [T]he new immigration may have an adverse fiscal impact because recent waves participate in welfare programs more intensively than earlier waves; ... [T]here exists a strong correlation between the skills of immigrants and the skills of second-generation Americans, so that the huge skill differentials observed among today's foreign-born groups become tomorrow's differences among American-born ethnic groups" (1513).

Gans (1992) proposes a similar explanation for the failure of assimilation. According to him, assimilationist theory was first developed "in connection with the southern and eastern European immigration [to the United States] of about 1880 to 1925," which was "during a time in which the economy was growing more or less continuously, especially with the employment of immigrant physical labour" (174). This situation no longer exists as the economy is now facing serious problems, and most immigrants are visible minorities coming largely from non-European countries. Sanchez (1997), on the other hand, argues that the economic insecurity felt by Americans has led to the rise of a "racialized nativism" directed at recent immigrants. On the same point, Huber and Espenshade (1997, 1037) argue that "the tolerance for immigrants has waned in the last two decades." These developments do undoubtedly have the potential to limit opportunities available to recent immigrants, which means that their paths deviate from the path predicted by classic assimilationist theory. Such a deviation is well reflected in the research topics of recent interest: "segmented assimilation" (Zhou 1997), "second-generation decline," and "bumpy-line assimilation" (Gans 1992).

In addition to the changed source countries of immigrants, their composition has transformed, making assimilation a less likely scenario. According to Huntington (2005), the feasibility and likelihood of the assimilation of previous waves of migration (up to the late 1960s) was facilitated by the fact that most immigrants were coming from Europe, through a "self-selection" process involving a willingness to assimilate and to confront the risks, costs, and uncertainties of migration; arriving from many countries (as opposed to large numbers coming from a few countries); and dispersing into various neighbourhoods. They also came in discontinuous waves, allowing them to integrate into a host population that shared a common and reasonably clear identity. Over the past three decades, according to Huntington, almost all of these features faded away. More and more immigrants are now arriving from non-European countries whose cultures are distinct from those of the host societies. Thanks to significant improvements in communication and transportation technologies, immigrants neither have to treat their migration as a one-way journey nor view their integration into host societies as their only option. Immigration waves are relatively continuous now, allowing for a constant reinforcement of immigrants' original culture and language. And, due to a higher degree of residential segregation, a lot of immigrants live in the vicinity of other immigrants from their home countries and have minimal contact with the mainstream population.

The above challenges to the assimilation process created two conflicting responses. The first was a recommendation that, with the increasing cultural and ethnic diversity of immigrants, host societies should adopt a multiculturalist policy to celebrate this new diversity (this is the main theme of the politics of recognition, discussed below). The second response, ironically, involved a return to the assimilationist perspective, the difference being that this time assimilation was prescribed rather than described. In other words, the old incarnation of assimilation was as a concept that could be used to explain the process of the integration of immigrants, while its new incarnation is as an ideology to be implemented and followed.

The most explicit version of this reincarnation is expressed by Samuel Huntington. In his last book, *Who Are We?*, Huntington (2005) argues that, to undo the damage done by this new diversity, the United States has to return to its British Protestant heritage and make it the foundation of its new national identity. While Huntington's recommendation remains largely at the theoretical level in the United States, in other places it has entered the practical level and has started informing policies. One example is the approach adopted by France towards its Muslim immigrants, but the most egregious example is what occurred in the small community of Herouxville in Quebec, Canada, where the residents announced that the new immigrants to their community should first sign a "contract" indicating their willingness to abide by the cultural values of the host community (Municipalité-Hérouxville 2010). While no specific group was mentioned in this declaration, the listed "undesired" values and practices were clearly perceived to be those associated with Muslim immigrants.

A major problem with the prescriptive version of the assimilationist perspective is that, even if immigrants adopted it they would not necessarily be accepted by the host population. As an example, one can look at one indicator commonly used to measure the degree of immigrants' willingness to assimilate into American society: the willingness to work hard and to improve one's life through disciplined work. Assume that an immigrant fully embraces this principle and, through hard work, creates for himself and his family a socio-economic status that is way higher than that of the average person in the host population. Would that trigger (1) a more positive reception on the part of the host population or (2) a feeling of being threatened? There is ample evidence pointing to the latter possibility – for example, the burning of businesses owned by Koreans during the 1992 Los Angeles riots, the negative attitudes towards working immigrants held by some low-income individuals (e.g., the perception that they steal jobs), and the professional jealousy that is often aimed at successful immigrant professionals.

One example of how such feelings relate to Muslims can be found in a survey conducted by the Pew Research Center (2007, 35). When Muslims were asked whether, since the 11 September 2001 tragedy, their lives had become more difficult, those who reported the highest percentages of difficulty were not the unemployed, uneducated, or unestablished; rather, they were those with the highest likelihood and strongest indicators of assimilation into American society – those with postgraduate degrees (65 percent), those with household incomes of $100,000 or more (68 percent), those who had arrived before 1990 (57 percent), and those in the eighteen- to twenty-nine-year-old age group (58 percent). In other words, the wave of anti-Muslim sentiment that surfaced in the United States after 9/11 seems to have targeted the most assimilated segments of the American Muslim population.

All these things suggest that assimilation alone does not have the capacity to adequately address the relationships between immigrant minorities and the majority. At best, what the prescriptive assimilationist perspective seems to accomplish is not the full-blown incorporation of immigrants but, rather, their adoption of the language, culture, and lifestyle preferences of the majority – an adoption whose purpose is to make life easier for the mainstream population rather than to create a more integrated society. This is perhaps why, as soon as immigrants are perceived as a threat to the job security and mental peace of the host population, they receive harsh treatment by that population, no matter how well-assimilated they might be.

Politics of Recognition (Cell 2)
The multiculturalism policies that were implemented in various Western countries during the last two decades of the twentieth century were, in one way or another, informed by the theoretical premises of what was later

known as the *politics of recognition*. The term was coined, and its underlying philosophy best articulated by, Charles Taylor (1992, 1994), who argues for the recognition of one's cultural and ethnic heritage as a part of one's human rights. In his words: "Recognition is not just a courtesy; it is a vital human need ... There is a certain way of being human that is my way, original, and it can be lost due to outward conformity and an instrumental stance towards oneself" (Taylor 1992, 26).

Speaking from a liberal communitarian viewpoint, as well as from a political philosophy background, Taylor argues that such recognition should be implemented at the level of public policy and discourse, and he sees the state as the main agent for accomplishing this. Alongside Taylor, people such as Will Kymlicka (1989, 1995, 2005) elaborate on the concept of recognition and also attempt to expand multiculturalism from a national to an international focus.

Partial evidence for the positive impacts of the politics of recognition has been found in the relatively better experiences of Muslims in Canada. Comparing Canada with Britain, for instance, two studies specifically attribute the former's favourable environment to the country's recognition-based multiculturalism policy. McGown (1999) compares the integration of Somali Muslim communities in Toronto and London, and finds that the Somalis living in Canada had a much easier time settling and integrating into the mainstream of the host society than did those living in England. She attributes this to a fundamental difference in what she calls the "political cultures" of the two countries:

> the culture of Multiculturalism has permeated the Canadian psyche and has become such a part of the political culture of the country ... Clearly this is aided by Canada's consciousness of its newness as a nation ... Canada's is an entirely immigrant population, with the exception of its Aboriginal population ... [O]ne of the side effects of Multiculturalism as official policy has been the recognition that an immigrant's head start of a couple of hundred years does not grant his descendants a greater legitimacy in the public or political order. (188)

The end result of this difference in the political culture, according to McGown, is that the Somali Muslims living in Toronto feel more comfortable than those living in London, who display more anger and other negative emotions about their lives. Despite the different languages – McGown's being more anthropological, Taylor's more philosophical – their underlying orientations to this issue are fundamentally similar. In both, the emphasis is on macro-scale policies revolving around the recognition of minorities, which, in turn, results in a less stressful and more comfortable environment for those minorities.

Modood (2007) finds similar differences between Canada and the United Kingdom, both in terms of the treatment of minorities in general and of Muslims in particular. In his discussion of the challenges of multicultural-ism in Europe, he clearly points to Canada as one of the two "exemplars" of what he means by multiculturalism and that "should be borne in mind as the policy examples" (16). He criticizes Europeans for having "overlooked" Canada as a place "where multiculturalism has been accepted and worked as a state project or as a national project" (147).

Besides concerns about the possibility that the politics of recognition may cause societal fragmentation or undermine the rights of minorities within minorities, one commonly raised issue is that it may not easily com-bine with the development of national identity. Modood (2007) considers this challenge so important that he thinks the key to salvaging multicultur-alism is to reinforce it by linking it to national identity, an issue that has not been adequately addressed or even acknowledged by multiculturalists. This is reflected, for instance, in McGown, who acknowledges the higher level of comfort among Somali Muslims in Canada compared to those living in the United Kingdom but who fails to address the issue that such comfort does not necessarily result in a stronger sense of identification with Canada. Such identification is absolutely necessary for the development of a sense of "we-ness." Indeed, as some critics of Taylor's politics of recognition thesis suggest, such comfort may indeed work in the opposite direction – that is, it may very well strengthen minority identity at the expense of national identity. The key point here is the need to distinguish between *comfort* and *identification*, and to acknowledge that the factors creating the former do not necessarily bring about the latter.

Political Engagement: Moderate Muslim Response (Cell 5)

The essence of this political engagement approach to Muslim integration involves calling on Muslim immigrants to consider modifying their be-liefs so that they are more compatible with life in Western democracies and peaceful coexistence with non-Muslims. While there is some variation, most of the recommendations under this political engagement category share a belief in the need for Muslims to make some kind of change in their philosophical ideas, in their reading of their faith's history, and/or in their realization of the difference between life in a Muslim country and life in a non-Muslim country.

In its simplest form, this approach can be found in a body of Islamic theological debates known as *fiqh al-aqalliyyat* (law and jurisprudence of minorities). The biggest concern of the proponents of *fiqh al-aqalliyyat* is to make the lives of Muslims in non-Muslim countries easier and more compatible with the principles of Islam. Towards this goal, they focus their energies not on developing radically new conceptual frameworks to deal with the lives of Muslims in non-Muslim environments but, rather, on expanding existing frameworks to incorporate the daily issues and practical problems facing these Muslims.

In a book dedicated to this issue, Yousef al-Gharzawi (2005), an Egyptian Muslim scholar, provides an outline of the approach taken by promoters of *fiqh al-aqalliyyat* as well as a thorough list of the questions addressed:

- Questions related to the larger issue of living in non-Muslim countries and what it might require: "Is the presence of Muslims in western countries religiously justifiable or not? Is it allowed for Muslims to live in the non-Muslim countries, or not? If yes, how could this be reconciled with the religious teachings that imply otherwise? What is the religious verdict for such Muslims, who are concerned with the integrity of their faith, or that of their children, due to living in non-Muslim or non-moral environments? How about adopting the citizenship of those countries? [if that is allowed] Would it be against Islam to take the citizenship oath, in which Muslims have to declare their respect for the law and the system of the host countries? What is the religious instruction on compulsory military service in the armies of those countries, especially when they declare war against a Muslim country – should such Muslims disobey the state, or fight against their own Muslim brothers?" (al-Gharzawi 2005, 25)
- Questions related to the practical challenges of everyday lives, such as: "[Given the required Islamic slaughtering method,] what is the religious instruction on the meat that Muslims purchase in the market, or those served in restaurants? Should a Muslim inquire about them actively, or should they consider those kinds of meat to be fine and usable without asking? (al-Gharzawi 2005, 25-26)
- Questions related to working in places in which pork and alcohol are served, or opening a business that would have to sell those products, or accepting invitations to attend parties in which pork and alcohol are consumed. (al-Gharzawi 2005, 26-27)

• Questions related to civic matters such as marriage and divorce. For example, should they be conducted through the legal system of the host societies or through Islamic organizations? What is to be done in situations in which there is a conflict between the civic law and Sharia law, as is the case with polygamy or heredity? Is it permitted for Muslims to marry non-Muslims? (al-Gharzawi 2005, 27)

• Questions related to working with banking systems that charge and give interest, such as: Is it permitted to have saving accounts with them or use their mortgages? (al-Gharzawi 2005, 27-28)

• And, finally, questions related to participating in the political life of host countries, such as: Is it permissible to become members of the political parties and/or to support them? Or to form political parties and/or simply nominate people and/or vote for them? (al-Gharzawi 2005, 28)

Addressing the daily issues and practical challenges faced by Muslims living in non-Muslim countries has always been a concern for Muslim scholars, but what distinguishes the promoters of *fiqh al-aqalliyyat* from more traditional scholars is their acknowledgment of the realities of life in non-Muslim environments and the need to develop a distinct *fiqh* system, not just an extension of the existing one. Al-Gharzawi (2005, 29) illustrates this different approach: "Some of our scholars are very knowledgeable, but lack an understanding of the conditions of those Muslim minorities; it is not enough that the scholars give those Muslims instructions merely on the basis of what is in the religious references, without enough knowledge of their situations and adequate research on their needs and necessities." The traditional approach of such scholars, according to al-Gharzawi, has led some of them to simply "discourage Muslims from living in non-Muslim countries" (33), as opposed to engaging with the realities of their lives there.

In order to introduce a well-integrated system of *fiqh al-aqalliyyat*, al-Gharzawi suggests that Muslim scholars concerned with the issues of Muslim minorities should base their work on the following principles: (1) engage in creative thinking (*Ijtihad*), as opposed to simply following the instructions of previous religious scholars; (2) pay attention to the actual living conditions of Muslim minorities; (3) focus on the needs of Muslim communities, as opposed to thinking merely about individual Muslims; (4) try to find solutions that would make life easier, rather than more complicated, for Muslims; (5) reduce the religious requirements and expectations of Muslims who might live in "unfavourable conditions"; (6) treat the realization of an Islamic lifesytle as a "gradual process" rather than an all at once event; (7) attend to human needs and reduce religious requirements accordingly. According to al-Gharzawi, relying on these principles will allow for adequate flexibility and an increased level of pragmatism in the lives of Muslim minorities.

While challenging the traditional approach of Muslim scholars and going a long way towards accommodating the special circumstances of Muslim minorities, *fiqh al-aqalliyyat* proponents do not feel the need to change any fundamental Muslim understandings. To them, finding solutions to the problems of Muslim minorities does not require a rethinking of the basic premises of Islamic philosophy and/or the history of Islam. Just as the migrations at the dawn of Islam resulted in the expansion of the faith, so, according al-Gharzawi (2005, 33), today's migrations will do likewise.

Such a view, however, is not shared by all Muslim moderates. Some feel that there is a need to re-examine certain historical and/or philosophical premises of Islam, particularly as it relates to the interaction of Muslim minorities and mainstream populations in Western countries. Salim Mansur is one of these people, and he recommends reconceptualizing the history of Islam. His principal argument is that Muslims should free themselves from an understanding of Islam that is heavily based on the historical experiences and cultural tendencies of only a small segment of the world's Muslim population – that is, the Arabs. Salim argues that, while Arabs constitute less than one-fifth of Muslims worldwide, they present their understanding of Islam as the only "authentic" interpretation of the faith. According to him, it was the faith as practised by the first generation of Muslims after the death of Prophet Mohammad – all Arabs of the Arabian Peninsula – that laid the ground for "the template of historical Islam" and that today this template, "unrevised and resistant to revision by most Muslims, Arabs and non-Arabs, instructs them in the understanding and practice of their faith tradition" (Mansur 2009, 2).

The specific historical experiences of this small segment of Muslims, according to Mansur, resulted in Islam changing from being a personal faith to being "the collective identity of a people – in modern terms, nationalism" (5). So a Muslim's duty, according to this line of reasoning, is to liberate him/herself from the heavy weight of this history and to change Islam from being a nationalistic force back to being a personal faith. This has led Mansur to celebrate what he calls "the quiet existence of Sufi Muslims" as the "right Islam," manifested through its "emphasis on the right conduct of Muslims

as individuals, and in repudiating the bigoted thinking based on the tri-
umphal view of Muslim history claiming Islam as superior to all other faith
traditions" (8).

One issue of interest to many moderate Muslims in the West, including
Mansur, is that of the uneasy relationship between Muslims and Jews. The
significance of this issue stems from the fact that this relationship has affected not only the prospect of peace in the Middle East but also the
possibility of peaceful coexistence between Muslims and non-Muslims in
Western secular democracies. Various Muslim scholars have suggested
different ways out of this problem. Mansur, for one, tries to show the common origins and shared features of Judaism and Islam, and to highlight
those parts of the Quran that ask Muslims to display a different – much
more respectful – treatment of Jews. Such elements had informed Muslim
practices in the past, as is evident in the experiences of Muslims in Spain.

Along the same line, but with a slightly different approach, Tarek Fatah
(2010), another moderate Muslim activist in Canada, identifies anti-Jewish
sentiments among Muslims as one of the sources of tension in the relationship between Muslims and Westerners, whether living in different countries
or within the same country. He questions the validity of what he calls an
anti-Jewish legend that informs the Muslim psyche:

> Where anti-Semitism in Europe has its roots in Christian mythologies that
> depicted the Jews as a dark and demonic force, responsible for the murder
> of the Son of God, Judeophobia in the Arab world stems from a completely
> different legend. Modern-day Muslims hold anti-Jewish prejudices not
> because their Prophet Muhammad was a victim of the Jews, but because he
> vanquished them in a decisive battle in Medina. And so I will challenge the
> primary legend of Islamic history that has made the killing of Jews literally
> an act of Sunnah, the practice of the Prophet. (Fatah 2010, xxiii)

Irshad Manji is also often viewed as a moderate Muslim voice in Canada. In her numerous TV appearances, contributions to the print media,
and, particularly, in her bestselling book *The Trouble with Islam*, Manji
provides a long list of problems that exist in the Muslim world. These range
from issues related to human rights, gender (in)equality, and dogmatism to
global issues such as Middle East conflict and the events of 9/11. As a solution to all these problems in/with Islam, Manji (2005) calls for the initiation
of what she terms "project *Ijtihad*." Defining the Islamic term *Ijtihad* as free
and critical thinking, Manji argues that this project's main mandate is to

offer a new interpretation of Islamic principles – one that is more compatible with the realities and sensibilities of today's world.

Like many other moderate Muslim voices, Manji has been criticized by more traditionally oriented and conservative Muslims; however, unlike them, she has also received criticism from other moderate Muslims. She is often accused of offering simplistic accounts of various problems, giving one-sided and unfair critiques of Muslims, and suggesting new interpretations of Islamic principles without being qualified to do so (e.g., without having a basic knowledge of Arabic as "the language of Islam"). Indeed, there are many problems with her work (e.g., suggesting DNA tests to settle the Palestinian-Israeli conflict, highlighting the social ills in Muslim communities without providing any critical view of social ills in Western democracies, and misrepresenting the concept of *Ijtihad* – which, in the Islamic context, refers to reasoning pertinent to the application of Islamic principles to contemporary issues – as equivalent to universal critical thinking). Manji's approach has damaged her connection with Muslims, and, as a result, her work is not very influential among them.

Probably Manji's most fatal oversimplification is to equate Islam with Muslims and then to treat Muslims as monolithic. This led to another moderate Muslim woman, Anar Ali, calling on Manji not to speak for her. Citing Manji's complaints about how the non-Muslim world generalizes about Muslims, Ali argues that Manji commits the same mistake from within. Ali (2007, 102) writes that, despite their very similar backgrounds, their experiences of Islam are quite different: Ali's is characterized by openness to other faiths, free thinking, and gender equality, while Manji's is not. After all, Ali writes, "there are one billion Muslims in the world." Despite these critiques from within the Muslim community, Irshad Manji is still considered as a moderate Muslim voice, albeit primarily by non-Muslims.

Akbar Ahmed is another moderate Muslim voice and a strong promoter of inter-faith dialogue in the United States. In a recent work, *A Journey into America*, Ahmed (2010) acknowledges the fact that more and more articulate Muslim moderates are appearing in the mainstream media – figures such as Fareed Zakaria, Irashad Manji, Reza Aslan, and Eboo Patel – but that these moderate voices do not enjoy large support from the Muslim communities, partly because they are viewed either as secular or as minority voices. He urges Muslim leaders to try to "improve their community's self-image" (447).

Among his recommendations to American Muslims, Ahmed (2010, 449) suggests that they learn from the experiences of the Jewish and Mormon communities how "to balance their religious and American identities." They also need to remember that, before they can secure mutual respect and friendship with Americans, Muslims must realize that "Americans feel the same intense loyalty towards America as Muslims do towards Islam" (451).

The most systematic and theologically sophisticated account of Muslim minorities from a Muslim perspective, however, comes from Tariq Ramadan, the renowned scholar of Islamic Studies. Ramadan calls on Muslims living in the West to rethink the contents of their faith in response to the realities of their lives in their new homes. The premise of this rethinking should be, he argues, to view Muslim life in other countries as a totally new phenomenon and not as a special circumstance and temporary deviation from "the real life" in home countries. Viewed this way, the realities of this new life require original thinking and a reformulation and reapplication of the basic concepts of Muslim faith. To do this, according to Ramadan, Muslims need to stop seeing themselves as a minority far from home or as diasporas whose physical presence is in one society and whose intellectual and emotional presence is in another. According to Ramadan, these unhelpful views are found in *fiqh al-aqalliyyat* (law and jurisprudence of minorities).

For Ramadan (2004, 7), *fiqh al-aqalliyyat* only makes it more likely that Muslims living in non-Muslim countries will "remain forever on the margins" (7). Instead, he suggests that "Western Muslims" free themselves from the implications of *fiqh* and become "intellectually, politically, and financially independent [from Muslim countries, and then] ... think for themselves, develop theses appropriate to their situation, and put forward new and concrete ideas" (6).

Ramadan (2004, 22) suggests that Muslims create an alternative *fiqh* by identifying and distinguishing "the essential principles (*al-usul*) from secondary injunctions (*al-furu*)" of Islam, with the understanding that it is only the former that is fixed and universal, with the latter being flexible and subject to interpretation:

> There is one Islam, and the fundamental principles that define it are those to which all Muslims adhere, even though there may be, clothed in Islamic principles, an important margin allowed for evolution, transformation, and adaptation to various social and cultural environments. Western Muslims, because they are undergoing the experience of becoming established in new societies, have no choice but to go back to the beginning and study their points of reference in order to delineate and distinguish what, in their

religion, is unchangeable (*thabit*) and what is subject to change (*mutaghayir*), and to measure, from the inside, what they achieved and what they have lost by being in the West. (9)

What he then lists as essential and unchangeable in Islam are those elements that inform a broad philosophical orientation to life as well as the contents of personal religious practices – *al-ibadat* – which aim at personal spiritual purification. The secondary, changeable, and historical elements – which he calls *ejtemaiyat* – are mostly related to the communal and social lives of Muslims in various societies and circumstances and, hence, are subject to interpretation and diversity:

> In the area of religious practice (*al-ibadat*) ... the texts ... were the only ultimate reference because the revealed rites are fixed and not subject to human reason ... and the margin for interpretation is virtually nil. In the wider area of human and social affairs, the established methodology is the exact opposite: [here] everything is permitted except that which is explicitly forbidden by a text ... Thus, the scope for the exercise of reason and creativity is huge ... people have complete discretion to experiment, progress, and reform as long as they avoid what is forbidden. (Ramadan 2004, 35)

According to Ramadan, Muslims have an arsenal of theological and jurisprudential concepts to utilize in exercising discretion in the realm of human and social affairs. This arsenal includes concepts such as *Fatwa* (a legal decision, involving the application of a general principle to specific circumstances), *Ijtihad* (a process of thinking and reasoning whose purpose is to apply a general principle to circumstances and issues for which no clear instruction is found in the texts), and *Maslaha* (which considers the common good as the basis of judgment). These three concepts are related: religious authorities and scholars issue *Fatwa*s based on principles known or inferred through *Ijtihad*, and one such principle is *Maslaha* (the common good of Muslims and/or the broader community).

Guided by these concepts, Ramadan goes on to formulate a few ideas that bear directly on the issue of Muslim integration into non-Muslim majority countries in Europe and North America. Three of these ideas are particularly relevant and innovative. The first involves his revision of the binary concepts of *dar-al-Islam* (abode of Islam) and *dar-al-harb* (abode of war), which have long informed Muslims' perception of the political geography of the world in which they live. Ramadan argues that Muslims were either living in the abode of Islam, which required them to abide by the law and participate in community, or in the hostile territory of the abode of war, which required no commitment. Ramadan suggests that the West, long perceived as a part of *dar-al-harb*, needs to be considered as a third category – that is, *dar-al-dawa* (abode of invitation to God), which resembles the situation of Prophet Mohammad and his followers in Mecca who lived as a minority before migrating to Medina and forming an Islamic state.

Ramadan's second idea involves his characterization of what constitutes a "Muslim identity" for "Western Muslims." Here, he suggests four elements: (1) faith, or belief in the Creator; (2) understanding, of the texts and of the socio-cultural environments in which they live; (3) education, or the transmission of faith to their children and others close to them; and (4) action and participation (i.e., the articulation of faith-consistent behaviour.) According to Ramadan, none of these elements conflicts with life in a non-Muslim country.

Ramadan's third idea involves his responses to some of the major questions in the minds of "Western Muslims," mostly revolving around how their commitment to Islam could be reconciled with loyalty to and engagement with non-Muslim societies. An underlying element of his responses is his emphasis on the fact that loyalty to any community, including the Muslim community (*ummah*), has to be consistent with the principle of justice and that a Muslim's decision to live in a non-Muslim society is implicitly based on a moral and social contract, by which he or she has to abide. In his words:

> It is clearly in the name of respect for the Islamic teachings of the *Sharia* that Muslims are able to live in the West and that they should respect the law of the country. So, in other words, Islamic law and jurisprudence *command* Muslim individuals to submit to the body of positive law enforced in their country of residence in the name of the tacit moral agreement that already supports their very presence. (Ramadan 2004, 95 [emphasis in original])

The above recommendation, of course, should not be taken to suggest passive acceptance of the norms and rules of the countries in which Muslims reside. Ramadan thinks that Western Muslims have every right to fight for justice and a living condition close to what Islamic teachings demand from them. However, he makes it very clear that such efforts should be taken only within the legal framework of the host countries and that Muslims should work "within the limits of what the law allows in order to find an adaptation as close as possible to the teachings of Islam" (Ramadan 2004, 95).

The Atheist Response

The atheist response – which finds its most popular formulation in the works of writers and speakers such as Sam Harris, Christopher Hitchens, Daniel Dennett, Richard Dawkins, and Ayaan Hirsi Ali – is a rather difficult one to categorize. For one thing, it was initially formulated in reaction to global issues involving Muslims and not specifically to Muslim immigrants. Although these people have talked extensively about issues relating to Muslim minorities, any discussions about immigrants have come mostly as a byproduct of their initial concern. Another source of difficulty in categorizing this approach lies in the fact that its proponents call for some sort of reformulation and reinterpretation of Islam – and, on that account, one may quickly place them in the category of moderate Muslims – but they are neither religious nor necessarily from a Muslim background. The last source of difficulty is the fact that, like assimilationists, the atheists call for Muslims to adopt the culture of host societies; however, that culture is defined not in terms of specific ethno-religious cultures (as Huntington suggests) but, rather, in terms of a return to the values of modernity and rationality. Despite these difficulties, the atheist approach to Muslim integration might be considered an off-shoot of the assimilationist approach as the two have many elements in common.

The label "atheism" suggests, as it should, that the proponents of this approach see religion as the root of the problems to be addressed. Sam Harris (2012), for instance, argues that his criticism of Islam, as of any other religion, "is aimed at its doctrine and the resulting behavior of its adherents," and that he is not "talking about races of people, or nationalities, or any other aspects of culture." This is a point that is also mentioned by Hirsi Ali (2010, xvii) when she describes her gratefulness for her success in escaping Somalia and other places, "where the affairs of men are conducted according to the dictates and traditions of faith." The task these authors define for themselves is to show the inconsistencies within faiths, along with the anti-modern elements of theologies, which are unacceptable by today's standards of rationality.

This may leave the impression that these authors tend to criticize various faiths and religions equally. However, one quickly detects a special attention to Islam. In the case of Hirsi Ali, the emphasis on Islam can be traced to the fact that she fled an extremely traditionalist and religious Muslim society as well as her Muslim parents. Others are led by a notion of some sort of clash of civilizations. Harris (2004, 109), for instance, argues that he focuses on Islam because: "We are at war with Islam. It may not serve our immediate foreign policy objectives for our political leaders to openly acknowledge this fact, but it is unambiguously so." He adds that the problems with Islam are not only present in its extremist interpretations but also in its moderate ones: "It is not merely that we are at war with an otherwise peaceful religion that has been 'hijacked' by extremists. We are at war with precisely the vision of life that is prescribed to all Muslims in Koran" (ibid.).

The atheist approach looks very similar to the assimilationist one in that it puts the onus on minorities – that is, Muslims – to take the initiative to change their situation. Atheists are also similar to moderate Muslims in that they promote a rereading of the Muslim faith by Muslims themselves. However, their suggested solution widens the gulf between themselves and moderate Muslims. In essence, atheists suggest the need for a thorough transformation of the Muslim faith not by replacing the more "fundamentalist" elements with more "moderate" ones but by doing away with the principles of Islam altogether. Harris (2004, 110) puts this most explicitly: "A future in which Islam and the West do not stand on the brink of mutual annihilation is a future in which most Muslims have learned to ignore most of their canon."

On the more specific issue of Muslim minorities living in Western countries, Hirsi Ali (2010, xxii) predictably criticizes multiculturalism as a force that will prevent Muslims from seriously engaging in rethinking the contents of their faith:

To be blunt, their efforts to assist Muslims and other minorities are futile because, by postponing or at best prolonging the process of their transition to modernity – by creating the illusion that one can hold on to tribal norms and at the same time become a successful citizen – the proponents of multiculturalism lock subsequent generations born in the West into a no-man's-land of moral values.

Interestingly enough, while they view the irrationality of religion as a source of problems and regard the multiculturalism policies of Western states as futile, both Harris and Hirsi Ali display a soft spot for Christianity. Harris (2012), for instance, acknowledges that there are some secular Muslims of good will who would like to improve the situation of Muslims in general, but they are virtually silent "because they have nothing to say that makes any sense within the framework of their faith ... *That* is the problem we must keep in view. And it represents an undeniable difference between Islam and Christianity at this point in history." Hirsi Ali (2010, xxiv) goes further and argues that one of the institutions that could help to solve the problem is "the community of Christian churches." This is so because:

> This modern Christian God is synonymous with love. His agents do not preach hatred, intolerance, and discord; this God is merciful, does not seek state power, and sees no competition with science. His followers view the Bible as a book full of parables, not direct commands to be obeyed.

Harris's and Hirsi Ali's views on Islam and Christianity further blur the distinction between the atheistic approach and the assimilationist approach to Muslim integration. At a minimum, an emphasis on the centrality of the host culture indirectly reveals a preference for Christianity – and sometimes even directly (e.g., Samuel Huntington's preference for "Protestant British" culture).

The above linkage between the atheist and the assimilationist approaches renders the former subject to the critiques previously discussed in that it ignores the fact that the assimilation of immigrants does not necessarily result in their being accepted by host societies. Further, the atheistic approach is on particularly shaky ground because it assumes that the behaviour of the adherent of a religion is the direct result of the doctrine of that religion. In assuming such a direct, one-way linkage, supporters of this approach reduce the complexity of human behaviour to a single variable. Not only that, but the inconsistencies they display between their treatment of Islam and their treatment of Christianity may be seen as an ethnocentric romanticization of the modernity and secularism of the West. Harris (2012) best demonstrates this self-assured ethnocentrism when he discusses the need for Muslims to change their attitudes: "These attitudes must change. The moral high ground here is clear, and we are standing on it."

Despite their differences, the main approaches to Muslim integration into host societies share certain features that seriously limit their effectiveness. These are discussed in the following chapter.

PART 2

CONCEPTUAL FRAMEWORK

4

The Fundamentals

Limitations of Existing Responses

The previous chapter introduces some of the main responses to the issue of the integration of minorities and immigrants in general and of Muslims in particular. These responses vary greatly in terms of their ability to adequately explain the problem and in their capacity to offer any tangible solutions. I now discuss three problems with those responses: (1) they treat identities as fixed entities; (2) they restrict the search for solutions to the cognitive and behavioural domains; and (3) they view integration merely as a product of macro-institutional policies.

Treating Identities as Fixed Entities

Until very recently, identity was predominantly conceived of as fixed. As a consequence, the task of the integrating immigrants, Muslim or otherwise, was understood as an effort to find a way to reconcile two identities: that of immigrants and that of the host society. In doing so, some argued that minorities needed to shed their "old" identities in favour of the identity of the majority; or, alternatively, that the majority should respect and acknowledge minorities' identities and allow them to keep them. In a compromise solution, some suggest that members of minority and majority groups sit down together and initiate a dialogue that would help them realize how much their two identities have in common.

It is true that, by suggesting that minorities should adopt the majority's identity, the proponents of the assimilationist view are indeed accepting the possibility of an identity change. However, they still see identities as discrete categories that one either has to adopt or to drop altogether, without being able to pick and choose various elements from different categories. They also view identity as the product of a conscious individual decision rather than as a product of a holistic existential experience.

Restricting the Search for Solutions to the Cognitive and Behavioural Domains

Most of the scholars discussed in the previous chapter assume that the behaviour of Muslims is influenced by the content of their religious beliefs; hence, only a change in those beliefs will lead to a change in behaviour. Here, they commit the double fallacy of reductionism and essentialism – fallacies that are committed by many conservative as well as progressive thinkers.

In the case of Muslim scholars, part of the reason for this tendency to reductionism and essentialism lies in a disciplinary bias resulting from their involvement with Islamic studies, with its heavy focus on the content of Islamic faith rather than on a multidimensional sociological approach to analysis. Such a bias is most evident in Ramadan's (2007) contribution to a special issue of the magazine *Academic Matters* devoted to the topic of religion in universities. In this article, he expresses his dissatisfaction with the fact that the most recent wave of interest in Islamic studies has been accompanied by a focus on social and political issues surrounding Muslims at the expense of the study of "religious thought proper." He calls for a return to the "right" approach, which would make use of "Islamic legal heritage (*fiqh*), studies of the creed (*aqida*), philosophical progress (*kalam*), mystical thought (*sufi*), and social and political inquiry (*siasa sharia*)" (6).

Treating Integration Merely as a Product of Macro-Institutional Policies

In his most recent book, Amartya Sen (2009) offers a critique of the dominant approach to addressing the issue of justice – an approach that has implications for the current debates on multiculturalism, integration, and inclusion. He calls this approach "transcendental institutionalism," tracing it back to the works of thinkers such as Thomas Hobbes and Jean-Jacques Rousseau. The goal of this approach, according to him, is to identify "just institutional arrangements for a society" (5). In doing this, he argues, one loses the equally important non-institutional aspects in the process: "The nature of the society that would result from any given set of institutions must, of course, depend also on non-institutional features, such as actual behaviours of people and their social interactions" (6).

In response to transcendental institutionalism, Sen adopts a second highly comparative approach, which he refers to as a "realization-focused comparison"; that is, it is "concerned with social realizations (resulting from actual institutions, actual behavior and other influences)" (Sen 2009, 7). In this approach, things – including the integration process – are not as clear-cut, abstract, macro, and institutional as they are in transcendental institutionalism; rather, they are more fluid and versatile, with uncertain outcomes and changing identities, depending on how individuals are treated and how institutional policies are practised at the street level.

An example may help to illustrate Sen's argument. Take the employment equity legislation in Canada, which is an institutional measure to help fix inequalities facing minority groups – that is, women, Aboriginal Canadians, visible minorities, and those with disabilities – in the area of employment. The legal and institutional obligation of employers, according to this law, is that, if everything else is equal, the priority in hiring should be given to the aforementioned groups. However, things are never equal; or, if they are, it is neither easy nor straightforward to prove or disprove it. Thus, in spite of the spirit of the legislation, it leaves a lot of room for employers to make subjective decisions. An employer's likes or dislikes can therefore render irrelevant the "just institutional arrangement" that is at the heart of the employment equity law. So, in order for a just society to emerge, the institutional formula behind what constitutes "just arrangements" needs to be supplemented with similarly supportive formulae at the societal level.

Luckily, many of the thinkers in the field, including some of those discussed above, have shown signs of shifting towards Sen's position. In one of his most recent works, Charles Taylor, for instance, acknowledges that a merely political recognition may not provide the solution to diversity. In a co-authored report (Bouchard and Taylor 2008) on the state of majority-minority relations in the Province of Quebec, he argues that "the field of harmonization practices" is subject to two different routes: the "legal route" and the "citizen route":

> Under the legal route, requests must conform to formal codified procedures that the parties bring against each other and that ultimately decree a winner and a loser. The legal route is that of reasonable accommodation ... the second path ... is less formal and relies on negotiation and the search for

a compromise. Its objective is to find a solution that satisfies both parties. (Bouchard and Taylor 2008, 19)

The authors then argue that, for three main reasons, they "strongly favour recourse to the citizen route":

(a) it is good for citizens to learn to manage their differences and disagreements; (b) this path avoids congesting the courts; and (c) the values underlying the citizen route (exchanges, negotiation, reciprocity, and so on) are the same ones that underpin the Quebec integration model. (Bouchard and Taylor 2008, 19)

This clearly shows a shift away from a purely political-legal model for accommodating diversity. I return to this discussion in Chapter 3.

Tariq Modood (2007) also acknowledges the fact that multiculturalism policies, by themselves, will not solve the diversity challenge. He argues that the places in which multiculturalism has experienced success are those in which it has been linked to a nation-building project and to a shared national identity:

It does not make sense to encourage strong multicultural or minority identities and weak common or national identities; strong multicultural identities ... need a framework of vibrant, dynamic, national narratives and the ceremonies and rituals which give expression to a national identity. It is clear that minority identities are capable of having an emotional pull for the individuals for whom they are important. Multicultural citizenship requires, therefore, if it is to be equally attractive to the same individuals, a comparable counterbalancing emotional pull. (Modood 2007, 149)

In his most recent book, Ramadan (2010) seems to be moving in the direction of acknowledging that the shared sense of citizenship and belonging does not necessarily emerge through law and awareness; rather, it requires compassion, empathy, and mutual understanding:

Knowing how to make use of our rights is indeed important, but we also have to have some sense of our common humanity, a concern for others, a shared sensibility and a shared emotional life. We are talking about an ethics and a humanism that precedes (and succeeds) the law ... A common sense of belonging is not something that can be willed into existence; it is born of day-to-day life in the street, at school and in the face of challenges we all face ... The common law protects us, but it is common causes that allow us to respect and love one another ... In most circumstances, it is not dialogue between human subjects that changes the way they see others; it is the awareness that they are on the same path, the same road and have the same aspirations (and their interminable dialogue sometimes blinds them to this). (174-75)

The above shifts in thinking about the integration of immigrants in general and that of Muslim immigrants in particular, while welcome, still have not been fully integrated into the current body of scholarship on the issue. I now offer an alternative conceptual framework that is capable of integrating these various modes of thought.

Contours of an Alternative Conceptual Framework

The conceptual framework I propose treats identities as flexible; this recognizes not only the possibility of identity changes but also the possibility of carrying multiple and sometimes competing identities simultaneously. It also sees the true test of how well immigrants have been integrated into societies to be the strength of their emotional attachment to their new homes; this transcends the inadequacy of existing perceptions, which revolve around behaviours or knowledge. Finally, it considers the integration process to be heavily informed by the nature of social interactions between immigrants and the receiving population; this process results not only from institutional practices and policies but also from socio-economic actions. Due to the centrality of the concept of "interaction" in my conceptual framework, I refer to it as an *interactionist* perspective. Below, I elaborate on its various components.

Emotions as Predictors of Cognitive Judgments

The debate about what drives people's behaviours and attitudes has a long history in the social sciences. On one extreme there is the notion of "the rational agent," someone who weighs his/her options by analyzing their associated costs and benefits and then choosing the option that maximizes the benefits. This notion has long informed many theoretical approaches in various disciplines, including the "intellectualist" tradition in philosophy and "rational choice theory" in economics (Blume and Easley 2008), sociology (Coleman 1990), and religion (Stark and Bainbridge 1987; Stark and Finke 2000; Young 1997).

Recently, however, the validity of rational choice theory has come under criticism. In their *Choices and Chances*, Tepperman and Wilson (1996), for instance, argue for the "minimization of dissatisfaction" as opposed to the "maximization of satisfaction" as a viable and frequently adopted strategy guiding people's thoughts, decisions, and behaviours. Also, recent scholarship on the concept of social capital highlights that, even in the market, and even if the actor's intention is to play according to rational rules, the resulting behaviours are not always the most rational outcomes simply because of the imperfection of the markets (see Burt 1995). Critiques of rational choice theory have also been raised by other economists, including those in behaviourial economics and those who suggest that, because of the lack of knowledge about human motivations, the theory should be used only in explaining the behaviours of firms and not of individuals.

The most serious and convincing challenge to the rational choice perspective, however, comes from social psychological research. In a recent study, Schnall et al. (2008) ran an experiment in which the participants were asked to express their moral judgments about several different scenarios. While the participants were busy processing the information, the experimenters exposed them to various unpleasant things, such as the release of a bad smell, working in a disgusting room, and recalling a physically disgusting experience. The findings of this experiment indicate that the feelings resulting from those unpleasant experiences influenced the contents of the participants' moral judgments. According to these scholars, the findings of this experiment run contrary to the implications of the grand tradition of moral philosophy – manifested in the works of philosophers such as Immanuel Kant and John Stuart Mill – in which "the virtues of reason" and the need to choose "the correct course of action based on expected utility" are emphasized (1096). These results are in line with the views of David Hume: "Morality is determined by sentiment. It defines virtue to be whatever mental action or quality gives to a spectator the pleasing sentiment of approbation; and vice the contrary" (quoted in Schnall et al. 2008, 1096).

What, then, are the implications for a study of the integration of immigrants into host societies if one accepts that moral judgments and rational calculations could be influenced and/or undermined by the un/pleasantness of experiences? To answer this question, the reader needs to be reminded of a point made earlier in this chapter: the true indicator of immigrants' integration is their ability to develop emotional attachments to their new homes, as opposed simply to voting in elections or abiding by the country's laws and sense of history (which involve only the physical and cognitive components of their existence). Immigrants' emotional state of mind is closely related to the sentiments they develop in their new countries, and it is these that will inform the contents of their judgments about the receiving society and their place in it. The logical extension of this argument is that, in the absence of such pleasant feelings, chances are that immigrants will develop an attitude towards the receiving society that is not conducive to further integration.

This possibility was frequently brought up during face-to-face interviews conducted with several Muslim immigrants. When asked about the negative views of some Muslim immigrants towards their adopted homes, a male thirty-something Muslim immigrant from Pakistan who is now living in the Prairies put it this way:

> To me, the association with anything has to be pleasant. If it is not pleasant, you don't want to associate with that, whether it is a country, whether it is a book, whether it is a city, whatever it is.

Referring to the possibility that the presence of a general negative feeling might influence an immigrant's judgment about every experience he or she has in the new environment, the same immigrant said:

> The first question that comes to your mind, the first negative thought that comes to your mind is ... [that of] not liking that country. So, don't let a negative thought ... come in. You have to have a target/goal in mind. If you have a target, you will get there. If you keep focusing on little things – like the price of gas being too high, or not having enough "whatever" you used to – then, I think you will never succeed ... If your fundamental values are not in danger, then, I think associating yourself with the country you live in is of paramount importance.

The above interview highlights three important points: (1) due to challenges involved in migration experiences, immigrants are prone to an initially negative view of the host society; (2) such negative views are not necessarily permanent (i.e., they may be overwritten by more positive ones); (3) the key to switching from a negative to a positive view lies in immigrants' having a clear, attainable goal for their post-migration lives.

Thus, depending on how pleasant an immigrant's overall experience has been, he or she could perceive a specific economic outcome – financial success, for example – in two entirely different ways: success because of the host society or success in spite of it. Clearly, the former would lead to a much stronger sense of belonging to the host society than would the latter.

Significance of Interactions in the Social Domain

For a long time, the dominant modes of understanding social dynamics were grouped under "structuralism" (actions determined by broad institutional forces) and "agency-based" (actions determined by individual actors). More recently, efforts have been made to soften the extreme deterministic nature of the structuralist approach and the extreme voluntaristic nature of the agency-based approach. One such effort can be found in a broad theoretical framework known as the *relational* perspective, which starts with acknowledging the fluidity of social processes and the diversity of potential outcomes, none of which is inevitable (see Dépelteau 2008; Perry and Shotwell 2009; Tilly 1984, 1998, 2006, 2007).

In his study of several historical developments, sociologist Charles Tilly shows the usefulness of adopting a relational perspective. For Tilly, interaction does not have to occur between individuals: it can just as well occur between groups, classes, institutions, and nations. Seeing outcomes as the products of the contents of such interactions, one can do away with narrow deterministic views that attach a high degree of predictability to social processes.

In his attempt to fine tune the idea of justice as discussed by political philosophers, Amartya Sen (2009) comes very close to a relational perspective. In his preface to *The Idea of Justice*, he suggests the following three principles: (1) the importance of engaged reasoning for promoting justice; (2) a need to focus on the processes through which a just society can be achieved or approached rather than focusing on characterizing a perfectly just society (as most political philosophers have done); and (3) paying more attention to the behaviourial aspects of such processes as opposed to the institutional aspects, which, again, have been the focus of many political philosophers. In short, what he suggests is a shift of focus from social contracts to interactions.

The application of the above principles to the subject of our study suggests that the integration of immigrants into host societies, as a desired social outcome, should not be taken for granted. The extent and the nature of such integration depends on the nature of the relations developed between immigrants and the host society. It follows that such outcomes would vary from group to group and from one individual to another.

Social Interactions and Identity of Immigrants

Assuming that the desired outcome of the integration process for immigrants is (1) the development of a sense of belonging, (2) the surfacing of an emotional attachment to the host society, and (3) the formation of common identities with the majority, my argument is that the nature of immigrants' relations and interactions with the larger society and the majority population is the determining factor in what accounts for successful integration. The main axioms of this conceptual framework are:

- The strength of the attachment of immigrant groups to the larger society is correlated with the extent of overlap between the former's identities and the latter's national identity (Putnam 2007).
- Such overlaps are shaped by two sets of factors: (1) institutional factors, which have received more attention in the literature and include things such as in/equalities in gaining access to vital economic and political resources; and (2) situational factors – that is, relationships that take place at micro-levels (among individuals and groups) (see Callero 2003; Cerulo 1997; Howard 2000; Sanders 2002; Satzewich and Wong 2006).
- Situational interactions are particularly powerful in fostering a sense of common identity. Social contact among people of different ethnic/cultural backgrounds can shatter their preconceived negative stereotypes towards each other and, hence, generate new and common identities that will set new boundaries for in- and out-groups. This is the main premise of the social psychological hypothesis known as contact theory (see Allport 1979 [1954]; DeYoung et al. 2005; Dixon 2006; Emerson, Kimbro, and Yancey 2002; Marschall and Stolle 2004; McLaren 2003; Moody 2001; Pettigrew 1998; Powers and Ellison 1995; Sacerdote and Marmaros 2005; Sigelman et al. 1996; Sigelman and Welch 1993; Stein, Post, and Rinden 2000; Verkuyten 2005, 2007; Verkuyten and Kinket 2000; Verkuyten and Martinovic 2006; Verkuyten and Thijs 2002; Yancey 1999).
- Identity transformations occur through four possible mechanisms: (1) learning about the out-group and the correcting of misperceptions; (2) changing behaviours among the members of the groups involved, which, in turn, can modify their previous attitudes; (3) development of emotional and affective ties; and (4) weakening of ethnocentric views (Pettigrew 1998). Initial studies emphasized that such processes materialize only in situations marked by four key conditions: equal group status

within the situation; common goals; inter-group cooperation; and the support of authorities, law, or custom. One may justifiably argue that contact and social interaction alone do not necessarily bring about positive outcomes as people may dislike one another, particularly in the absence of the four above conditions. That is a valid argument, but there are two counter-arguments. First, even when the outcome of social interactions is negative, it is more likely to be based on personal likes and dislikes and personality conflicts than on stereotypical and categorical likes and dislikes. So, in these cases, the negative judgments about others remain limited to individuals and are not generalized to a larger group. This is a positive development in itself as it keeps alive the possibility of a different outcome based on a different social interaction. Such possibilities are not easy to come by when judgments are made primarily on the basis of stereotypical images. Second, more recently, Pettigrew and Tropp (2006) convincingly show the robustness of contact theory even when the four above-mentioned conditions are not fully met.

- Identity change does not necessarily mean the replacement of one identity with another; rather, people may have multiple identities, with one being dominant, depending on the circumstances. So identity transformation may very well be signified by a change in the "identities portfolio" of a group, minority, or majority (for a discussion of the same dynamics in nineteenth-century United States, Singapore, South Africa, Britain, and India, see Costa and Kahn 2003a, 2003b, 2006; Eng 2002; Haile, Sadrieh, and Verbon 2008; Kadir 2005; Sen 2006; Varshney 2001).

The significant positive impact that social contact can have on the creation of bonds between people of diverse backgrounds is clear in Putnam and Campbell's (2010) study of religion in the United States. Trying to explain how American society has solved what they called "the puzzle of religious pluralism – the coexistence of religious diversity and devotion" (550), Putnam and Campbell arrive at two interesting findings. First, the co-existence of religious diversity is attained through a high degree of "bridging" – that is, through including people of different faiths in one's social network. They believe that this kind of network leads to "a more positive assessment of other religious groups, even those that were not added to the friendship network" (532). They refer to this as the "spillover effect": "perhaps upon realizing that you can be friends with ... a member of a religious group you once viewed with suspicion, you come to reevaluate your perception of other religious groups too" (ibid.).

Second, Putnam and Campbell (2010) found that their respondents, in the process of shattering stereotypes concerning "others" as a result of increasing their level of contact with them, not only ignored scriptural teaching but also displayed a wide gulf between their beliefs and the beliefs of their clergy – the guardians of the official interpretation of scripture. This is an extremely important finding, and it corroborates a point I make earlier: the theological contents of a faith are not the only determinant of the behaviours of that faith's followers. For this reason, an attempt to fix the relationship between two faith communities cannot start with a call for a reinterpretation of their respective holy scripts; rather, it should start with changing the nature of the social relations that could inspire a believer to feel the need for such a reinterpretation. Trying to overcome this problem of cognitive dissonance, people may find it necessary not only to reinterpret parts of their faith but also to question and/or ignore certain elements of their scriptural teachings, all in favour of more moderate and inclusive teachings.

The Synthesis of Conceptual Approaches

Relating our discussion here to the critical review of the existing perspectives on integration described in Chapter 3, we are now able to extend the classification offered in Table 3.1 by adding Cell 8 – interaction/contact (the social) – under majority and minority agency. Table 4.1 shows the relative position of this added cell in relation to the ones suggested earlier.

By adding "interaction" to the "diversity" debate, my conceptual framework provides more flexibility to how research questions regarding the integration of immigrants into host societies are addressed. It allows us to examine how different interaction experiences may be related to different experiences of identity transformation. Some recent works in this area indicate the rising appeal of the relational approach in Canada (see, for instance, Arat-Koc 2006; Bouchard and Taylor 2008; Nesbitt-Larking 2008; Reitz 2009b; Reitz, Breton, Dion, and Dion 2009).

In using the above ideas to detect the patterns with regard to the integration of immigrants, I treat the whole process of integration as what Pierre Bourdieu refers to as a "field." Bourdieu uses this term to refer to a structured social space with some regularities, a history, and certain knowable properties. A field is defined as "a series of institutions, rules, rituals, conventions, categories, designations, appointments and titles which constitute an objective hierarchy, and which produce and authorise certain discourses and activities" (Webb, Schirato, and Danaher 2002, 21-22).

TABLE 4.1

Classification of perspectives on integration: Who, what, and where

		WHAT (nature of the problem/solution)		
		Cultural	Political	Economic	Social
WHO (agent of change)	Majority	❶ Cultural education/ anti-racism *(WHERE: Mind)*	❷ Politics of recognition *(WHERE: Mind-Soul)*	❸ Anti-discrimination *(WHERE: Body)*	
	Minority	❹ Assimilation/ exclusion *(WHERE: Body/Mind)*	❺ Political engagement *(WHERE: Body)*	❻ No welfare-dependency *(WHERE: Body)*	
	Majority and minority	❼ Inter-faith dialogue *(WHERE: Mind)*			❽ Interaction/ contact *(WHERE: Soul)*

Within each field there is the possibility of having several subfields – that is, segments of the broader social space that share the general properties of the field but have their own special subset of regularities. As one example of this kind of structure, Webb, Schirato, and Danaher (2002) refer to the field of professional sports, within which there are subfields consisting of the athletes, the managers, the organizing bodies, and so on. Another example is the field of the business world, which has subfields consisting of investors, CEOs, and regular staff. The concept of field is the Bourdieuian equivalent of structure, without the rigidity and inflexibility often associated with the latter.

I treat the process of immigration and integration as a field and that of Muslim immigration and integration as a subfield. Immigrants' experiences during and after migration illustrate certain relatively stable features, although these are bound to change with major demographic transformations in immigration dynamics. A close approximation of an immigration field may be found in John Porter's (1965) seminal work, *The Vertical Mosaic*. In his study, Porter ties the economic experiences of immigrants to the timing of their arrival, creating a social and occupational ladder with the Charter groups at the top, followed by other Western European immigrants,

Eastern Europeans, southern Europeans, and, finally, those coming from the developing world. While sharing many of these regular features, Muslim immigrants have certain experiences that are unique to them. These partly stem from international realties that relate to Muslims but not to other immigrants as well as from certain historical encounters between the Muslim world and the West. Recognizing the experiences of Muslims as a subfield allows for differential assessments of and responses to their situation, independent from the responses to the general immigrant population.

Having provided an overview of the fundamental concepts that guide my study, in the following chapters I expand them into testable hypotheses. In Chapter 5, I begin to discuss the specific case of Muslims in Canada.

5

Canadian Immigration and Muslim Immigrants
The "Field" and the "Habitus"

As I have said, I take a Bourdieuian approach to the integration of immigrants. The defining features of this approach consist of the use of interdisciplinary frameworks, eclectic theoretical perspectives, and mixed methodology (quantitative and qualitative). I also rely heavily on the concepts of "field" and "habitus," which Bourdieu coined in order to settle the long-time debates in social sciences over the relationship between agencies and structures. In many respects, the experiences of immigrants in Canada reveal the interaction between a field and a habitus, with the former referring to the tendencies and biases immigrants carry within themselves and the latter referring to the structural features of Canadian society. Below, I discuss the field of the Canadian immigration environment and the habitus of Muslim immigrants.

The Field

The most salient feature of the current Canadian immigration field is the absence of a regional or racial bias with regard to the type of immigrant admitted. This is an extremely important Canadian institutional feature, and it is the product of a series of changes in Canadian immigration law during the 1960s, whereby the point system replaced the systemic preference for European immigrants. This new system assigned heavy weight to education, language skills, work experience, and the ability to work in the Canadian job market, and this resulted in a significant increase in the number of professional and highly educated immigrants (as well as other immigrant classes) from non-European sources. This change resulted in the increase of (1) immigrants coming from Muslim countries and (2) the number of professional immigrants. The second increase was of enormous importance for the nature of the relationships between immigrants and the host society.

The increase in the number of highly educated immigrants supplied the Canadian economy with a pool of high-quality skilled workers who could easily enter the job market. This was a great advantage for a country looking to quickly satisfy its labour needs in a highly volatile economic environment. The open nature of the system (i.e., admitting immigrants on the basis of their qualifications as opposed to prearranged employment) made Canada a popular destination for various types of professionals: they were coming to operate in a democratic country that would value their skills and education. This development altered the Canadian immigration field in a fundamental way, transforming it from a "push-driven" environment to a "pull-driven" one.

It is well known that, for immigration to take place, there must be forces that either push immigrants out of their old home or pull them towards their new one. While these two sets of forces are present in any immigration experience, the relative weight of each could change, depending on circumstances. Whether an immigrant has been pushed out or pulled in has far-reaching implications for how that immigrant operates after arrival. In a predominantly push-driven situation, the decision to migrate is more heavily influenced by the undesirable conditions in the sending country. This means that these immigrants start the process of migration with an assumption that whatever is waiting for them in the receiving country will be better than what they are leaving behind. Push forces include severe economic recession, famine, war, and persecution as well as separation from members of their families. Clearly, refugees and family-class immigrants migrate more under the influence of push forces than of pull forces. On the other hand, skilled workers and highly educated professionals rarely migrate out of desperation; rather, they leave their countries of origin in search of better educational and employment opportunities as well as higher standards of living. In other words, they migrate voluntarily, with more information about their destination and higher expectations. Unlike refugees and family-class immigrants, immigrant professionals are more likely to choose the country of destination and, thanks to their human capital, to have the capability to move from one destination to another.

The shift of the Canadian immigration field from a push-driven to a pull-driven environment resulted in the arrival of immigrants who were more mobile and who had higher and more specific goals for their migration. For this type of immigrant, the decision to adopt the new country as home is not an automatic one: they choose to do so only if they feel that their expectations will be met. If not, they either choose to leave for another destination or return to their countries of origin. According to the data from the Longitudinal Survey of Immigrants to Canada, those drop-outs constitute about 10 percent of all immigrants. Another 80 percent keep to their initial intention of permanent residence in Canada (at least for the first four years, as covered by LSIC data). If their experiences are not positive, they are likely to become frustrated and, hence, develop little or no sense of attachment to their new country. Although initial disappointment can last a long time, with positive changes in the nature of their experiences, these immigrants may switch from a weak to a strong attachment. For post-1960s immigrants who are migrating under the influence of pull forces, the process of forming an attachment to Canada is often much more volatile and uncertain than it is for those migrating under push forces and is heavily dependent upon the nature of their experiences.

The Habitus

The higher level of expectations among immigrants in a pull-driven environment is part of a bigger package that, in Bourdieuian terminology, is referred to as a habitus (see Bourdieu 2005). Habitus is defined as "a system of durable, transposable dispositions which functions as the generative basis of structured, objectively unified practices" (Bourdieu 1979, vii). Habitus, according to Webb, Schirato, and Danaher (2002, 15), "constitutes Bourdieu's most ambitious attempt to ground and explain practices in terms of both specific and general socio-cultural contexts, rather than in terms of grand narratives of history (Marxism), psychoanalysis (the Oedipus Complex), structuralism (Levi-Strauss) or 'authentic being' (Heidegger)." The regularities seen in the social arena are the joint products of the relative stability of the properties of a field and the durable tendencies of a habitus.

In the context of our discussion, the notion of habitus accounts for the fact that immigrants in a pull-driven environment do not arrive as blank slates; rather, they carry with them not only a set of expectations but also the imprint of their pre-migration lives and experiences, advantages, tendencies, and preferences. When those expectations are not met, their perceptions about Canada and their level of attachment to their new home suffers.

FIGURE 5.1

Immigrant class and attachment to Canada, Wave 1 (six months after arrival), Wave 2 (two years after arrival), and Wave 3 (four years after arrival) (beta coefficients)

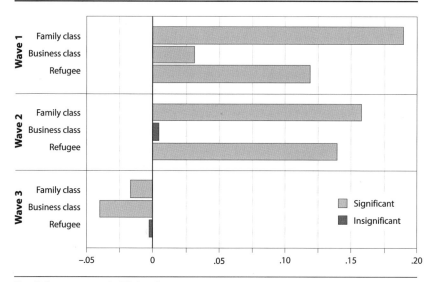

Note: Reference category is skilled workers.

Source: Statistics Canada, Longitudinal Survey of Immigrants to Canada, 2005.

As an illustration of this evolving phenomenon, one could examine the changes in the strength of the attachment to Canada on the part of different categories of immigrants. Figure 5.1 shows the levels of attachment reported by skilled workers, refugees, business-class, and family-class immigrants to Canada at three points during their first four years in the country: six months, two years, and four years after arrival. The figure reports the strength of attachment for three groups while using the fourth – skilled workers – as the baseline (or reference category).

Figure 5.1 shows that, in Wave 1 (six months after arrival), skilled-worker immigrants show the weakest level of attachment to Canada. This is interesting as this group consists of immigrants who have been admitted on the basis of their education and work skills. Refugees and family-class immigrants have been selected mostly for humanitarian reasons, and business-class immigrants have been selected for their financial resources. All three groups receive some kind of support in their first few months in Canada – refugees from sponsoring agencies, family-class immigrants from other family members, and business-class immigrants from their financial resources. Skilled workers are the only immigrants who have to rely on their work for survival. The fact that they are reporting the lowest level of attachment may be related to this fundamental difference in their economic situation and to many of them being unable to find requisite employment in those first months.

Figure 5.1 reports the same thing for these immigrants in Wave 2 (two years after arrival). Here, the pattern remains the same, except that the strength of attachment is somewhat reduced for refugee, family-class, and business-class groups. At this point, the refugees are beyond the one-year support they received from the sponsoring agencies, the family-class immigrants are settled and may have started looking for jobs, and business-class immigrants are through with their initial planning and are ready to hit the job market. The reduced levels of attachment for these three groups could very well be a reflection of the new economic realities in their lives.

Figure 5.1 also shows a very radical change in the position of these three groups in Wave 3 (four years after arrival). All three groups have switched to the negative zone – that is, they report much lower levels of attachment to Canada than do skilled workers. This could be the result of either a drop in the attachment levels of these groups or a noticeable increase in attachment for the skilled workers. In either case, it seems that the economic realities have become more favourable for skilled workers, resulting in their increased level of attachment to Canada. Interestingly enough, compared to skilled workers, business-class immigrants show the biggest drop in attachment in this time period. Refugees remain almost the same but their attachment to Canada is still stronger than that of family-class and business-class immigrants.

This highlights several points. First, the sense of attachment to Canada is far from stable; rather, it is an evolving phenomenon, influenced by the nature of immigrants' experiences in their new homes, particularly in their first few years after arrival. Second, the better-educated skilled-worker immigrants seem to have a slow start with regard to developing an attachment to Canada; however, over time, this rate increases in comparison to that of other categories of immigrants. Third, while the data do not necessarily show it, the fluctuations observed with regard to level of attachment seem to reflect the fluctuations in the economic experiences of the various groups of immigrants. Further analysis of the same data confirms this hypothesis, showing the strong parallel between having a job and feeling strongly attached to Canada (for a more elaborate discussion, see Kazemipur 2012).

As central as economic experiences are for the development of a sense of attachment to Canada among immigrants, they are not the only factors: social experiences also play a critical role here. Actually, in many respects, the nature of the economic experience is influenced by the presence or absence of a healthy state of mutual acceptance between immigrants and the native-born population. Clear evidence for this is found in a study by Oreopoulos (2009), in which six thousand resumes were sent to potential employers in Canada in order to determine the rates at which different groups of hypothetical applicants received invitations for job interviews. The study's most interesting finding is that, controlling for all technical aspects, the applicants with English-sounding first and last names received the most interview invitations by a considerable margin, followed by those with mixed English-foreign names, and only then by those with foreign-sounding first and last names. According to Oreopoulos: "Overall, the results suggest considerable employer discrimination against applicants with ethnic names or with experience from foreign firms" (5).

In sum, the strength of immigrants' attachment to their new homes seems to be a function of the interaction between field and habitus. A more or less accommodating environment in the receiving country, in interaction with higher or lower expectations among immigrants, can result in a variety of outcomes. Such outcomes, in turn, go through fluctuations as immigrants settle into their new homes. During this process, the immigrants' initial plans, expectations, and perceptions can be reinforced, completely invalidated, or modified. The process, therefore, is much more dynamic than it may appear.

The specific interaction of the Canadian immigration field and Muslim immigrants' habitus adds even more complexity to the above picture. One source of this complexity is the fact that a large number of Muslim immigrants come from the Middle East and the Indian subcontinent, regions particularly prone to and damaged by long and violent conflicts. This has a twofold effect on the Muslim immigrants' habitus. First, it has made the seeking of a peaceful environment an important reason for their migration to Canada – much more than is the case for other immigrants – as indicated by the LSIC data. Second, people in the sending regions tend to hold a negative view of Western countries, perceiving them as at least partly responsible for the problems and sufferings of those in the Muslim world. A cursory look at some weekly public opinion polls conducted by the website of Al Jazeera (in Arabic) clearly shows this anti-Western bias (for a listing of the polls conducted between 2002 and 2011, see http://www.aljazeera.net). While such polls do not reflect the opinions of the whole population, they do reflect the opinions of the younger, better-educated, and more internet-savvy segments of the population – the same demographic from which professional immigrants to Canada are selected.

Of course, the existence of anti-Western biases among the populations of Muslim immigrants' home countries does not automatically mean that the immigrants themselves carry these views. After all, if such immigrants were entirely comfortable with things in their home countries, they would have little reason to migrate. However, the mere presence of such views could provide them with a ready-made conceptual framework for trying to make sense of the difficulties and challenges they might face after immigration. In other words, they might attribute their challenges in Canada to the presence of anti-Muslim bias in the host population. Whether such a view is adopted or not depends on the nature of their experiences in Canada: it will be adopted only if their post-migration experiences appear to confirm its validity. If they do not, that view will start to break down.

An example of this dynamic can be found in the case of Maajid Nawaz. As a British citizen of Pakistani origin, Maajid Nawaz held strong anti-Western views and was an active member of an extremist Islamist organization. In the course of extensive travel, and while passing through Egypt, he was arrested and imprisoned for four years. While in prison, he abandoned his extremist Islamist views in favour of a new outlook – one that was open to a constructive dialogue between Muslims and the West. When, in a televised debate, he was asked about the main reason for this change of heart, he cited Amnesty International (see a video clip of this debate in Intelligent-Square 2010). Campaigns organized by non-Muslim activists in Western countries, their purpose being to get Nawaz out of prison, contradicted his previously held stereotypical image of Westerners. Nawaz's doubt about the validity of those stereotypes then led him to change his identity from an extremist Islamist to a moderate Muslim, and from an exclusivist anti-Westerner to an inclusivist citizen who promotes dialogue. In the same fashion, post-migration experiences may serve to confirm or refute the ideas to which immigrants have been exposed before migration.

The above dynamics run contrary to the simplistic assimilationist idea that the more immigrants become like the native-born, the stronger their level of attachment to their new homes. In this view, the attachment to one's cultural heritage and the attachment to Canada are two parts of a

FIGURE 5.2

Sense of belonging to ethnic group, by sense of belonging to Canada

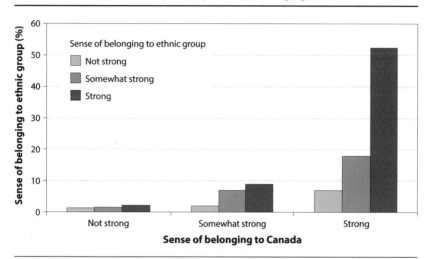

Source: Statistics Canada, Longitudinal Survey of Immigrants to Canada, 2005.

zero-sum game: more of one means less of the other. In the case of Muslim immigrants, the logical extension of this argument is that the stronger their attachment to Islam, the weaker their sense of belonging to Canada. The existing empirical evidence, however, refutes these claims.

Let us start with the first part of the assimilationist argument. Figure 5.2 shows the distribution of immigrants to Canada on the basis of the strength of their sense of belonging to their ethnic group as well as their sense of belonging to Canada. The graph shows that the overwhelming majority of immigrants not only report a strong sense of belonging to Canada but also that the strength of this sense of belonging rises when they have a strong attachment to their own ethnic group. In other words, the fact that immigrants are not forced to choose between these two in practice adds to their level of attachment to their new home. This could go some way to explaining at least part of the differences in the experiences of immigrants (including Muslim immigrants) in Canada as opposed to in some European countries.

Along the same lines, the experiences of Muslims show that their ability to freely practise their religion in Canada has the potential to result in a positive attitude towards, and a stronger attachment to, this country. In a face-to-face interview, a thirty-something male Ismaili Muslim immigrant from Pakistan now living in the Prairies speaks of this dynamic:

> I have suffered from prejudices more in the country of my parents,
> more in the country I was born in ... For myself, being a Canadian
> has given me a chance to practise my religion; [as] a faithful
> Canadian; as a Muslim, I feel more comfortable practising my
> religion here.

We should keep in mind that Ismaili Muslims in Pakistan constitute a minority under pressure and have occasionally suffered from violence. Being a pressured minority could certainly create a contrast between a person's home country and Canada and thus make it easier to appreciate the freedom she or he experiences in the latter. However, even those who were not religious in their home countries, or who became religious in Canada, report the same feeling, as is evident in the following:

> *Interviewee:* Like I said, I don't follow Islam because my parents
> were born Muslims; I follow Islam because I found it; and I found
> it because I was allowed to find it ...
> *Interviewer:* So, Canada helped with this?
> *Interviewee:* Oh, big time! ... I think, being in Canada, I am a lot
> more close [sic] to my religion than I was outside of Canada.
> *Interviewer:* Why is that the case?
> *Interviewee:* Just because there is a lot more freedom for me to
> believe in what I want to believe in; and for me to find my own
> way; and of course, there is a lot more opportunities here for me
> to profess my beliefs too.
>
> (Male immigrant in his late thirties, living in the Prairies)

One interesting aspect of this dynamic is the possibility that a rise of attachment to Islam after migration could be accompanied by a parallel rise of attachment to Canada. This became evident in the face-to-face interview with a female twenty-something Muslim immigrant from Lebanon, who stated that she was not a practising Muslim in her home country but that she had started "discovering" Islam here in Canada. As a result of her increased contact with Muslims from other Arab countries, this immigrant gradually shifted away from her Lebanese identity and adopted an Arab-Muslim identity. Simultaneously, she also incorporated into her identity elements from dominant Canadian culture and values, so much so that she now considers herself a "Canadian-Arab Muslim":

> I feel that the longer I live here, the more I am accustomed to
> Canadian values, and I accept a lot of it. And I feel that it can
> really be fused in with my Arab identity ... A Canadian Arab is one
> who appreciates other cultures as well, not just the strictly Arab
> [cultures] ... Things that I've taken and accepted from Canadian
> culture have become a part of me and that's something I don't want
> to give up. I won't give it up, even, let's say, if it's something that
> conflicts with Arab culture.

These examples show the fluid nature of the sense of attachment and of the identities that immigrants may develop after landing in their new homes. They also show that the process of developing such attachments and identities are heavily influenced by the receiving environment in the new country; the freedom to practise one's religion, for instance, can simultaneously strengthen the attachments to one's religion and to Canada. Further, healthy interaction with Canadian society can result in the immigrant's incorporating Canadian values into her/his identity.

In the above processes religion has a special place for the simple reason that it is capable of providing immigrants with a badly needed community. As has been noted in the literature, the loss of social networks and communal bonds is one of the heaviest burdens that immigrants experience as a result of their migration. The absence of social networks after migration not only deprives immigrants of some of the opportunities that are normally available through such networks (i.e., social capital) but also causes them to suffer from isolation and loneliness. The longing for a community, therefore, can draw immigrants to religion and/or result in their rediscovering their faiths. In some cases, even those with no prior religious conviction are attracted to religion, primarily for the communal bonds that it can offer.

An example of the communal role played by religion can be found in a recent study by Rashid (2011), in which she highlights the role that the discovery of mosques plays in the settlement process of some new Muslim immigrant women. She quotes one of these immigrants, who considers the discovery of the mosque to be a turning point in her postmigration life:

> I am [was] alone ... So it was like you don't have any sense of your country ...
> I felt lonely for, I would say, for first six-seven months till I went to the
> mosque. (Quoted in Rashid 2011, 130)

This immigrant found a great network of support in the religious community, especially during the difficult time of her pregnancy:

> I was new to that country, new to the system – didn't know anything. Then my – you know, God helped. Lots of people come and help us. A lady – she went to the mosque and she told the other ladies ... So she brought me food, and they cooked for me almost for one week. Then they kept taking us to the doctor appointment, driving us. I don't know how ... everything happens – I don't expecting that. (Quoted in Rashid 2011, 129)

In discussing the broad features of the Canadian immigration context (the field) and its interaction with Muslim immigrants (the habitus) I provide a context for the discussions to come in the following chapters. Both the field and the habitus have certain identifiable properties that strongly influence the experiences of Muslim immigrants in Canada.

To reiterate, this chapter has five major points: (1) the post-1960s immigration environment in Canada has become increasingly pull-driven (i.e., immigrants are attracted to Canada more because of what it can offer them than because of pressures in their home countries); (2) in a pull-driven environment immigrants are mobile and selective, and they arrive with high expectations; (3) the development of an attachment to Canada is related to whether immigrants' expectations are met – the closer their actual experiences are to their expectations, the higher the likelihood they will develop a strong attachment to Canada; (4) a crucial factor in developing a positive attitude towards Canada is the pleasantness of immigrants' post-migration economic experiences; and (5) also important in this process is the nature of immigrants' social experiences in their new homes.

Along with the information provided in Chapter 2 and the relational/interactionist approach discussed in Chapter 4, this chapter provides a sufficient conceptual framework for understanding the experiences of Muslims in Canada. Part 3 provides an empirical examination of the theoretical possibilities raised thus far.

MUSLIMS IN CANADA: FRONT STAGE

6

Canadian Muslim Lives

Diverse, Misunderstood, Gendered, Misrepresented

In this chapter and the next, I offer a general picture of the lives of Canadian Muslims, or at least of the most visible parts of those lives. I entitle this part of the book "Front Stage" because it describes the lives and experiences of Canadian Muslims without delving into their more complex and hidden relationships. The latter task is addressed in Part 4, which I entitle "Back Stage."

My focus here is on those aspects of the lives and experiences of Canadian Muslims that are poorly understood by the public and greatly misrepresented by the media. Specifically, I discuss four topics: (1) the enormous ethnic and cultural diversity of Canadian Muslims, (2) the poorly understood relationship between Islam and Muslims, (3) the special situation of Muslim women, and (4) the disproportional visibility and misleading portrayal of Muslims in the media.

Diversity of Canadian Muslims

In the heated discussions about the relationships between Muslims and others, quite often two simultaneous errors occur: (1) the minimization of the differences "among" Muslims and (2) the maximization of the differences "between" Muslims and others. The examples of the first error can be found in the arguments of people such as Bruce Bawer, who see Muslims as different from Christians in that the former are monolithic and have no moderate or liberal tendencies (for a discussion of Bawer's views, see Saunders 2012b). The popular perception of Muslims as a monolithic and homogeneous group masks not only the diversity of their political views and standpoints but also the enormous diversity of their ethnic and national backgrounds.

Addressing the image of a monolithic Muslim population is particularly important in the Canadian context because this image is in sharp contrast to the realities of the Canadian Muslim population, which is one of the most diverse Muslim populations in the world. While in many other immigrant-receiving countries the bulk of the Muslim population has come from only one or two relatively homogenous sources (e.g., Turks in Germany, North Africans in France, South Asians in the United Kingdom), recent data on Canadian immigrants (see LSIC) show that 70 percent of the Muslim immigrants who arrived in the early 2000s came from eight countries – Pakistan (26 percent), Iran (12 percent), Morocco (9 percent), Algeria (8 percent), Bangladesh (6 percent), India (5 percent), Lebanon and the United Arab Emirates (about 3 percent each). This high rate of diversity contrasts not only with other immigrant-receiving countries but also with other immigrants arriving in Canada. In the same cohort of immigrants arriving in the early 2000s, for instance, more than 70 percent of those from Eastern Religions as well as those who reported no religious affiliation came from only two countries; 75 percent of Orthodox immigrants came from four countries; about 60 percent of Jewish immigrants came from only two countries; and more than 35 percent of Catholics from only one country. Protestants comprise the only other religious group that is as diverse as Muslims.

A corollary of the popular (mis)perception regarding the homogeneity of the Muslim immigrant population is the false equation between Muslim and Middle Easterner. The breakdown of the Canadian Muslim population by national origin shows the inaccuracy of this perception as well. While Muslims coming from the Middle East make up only about one-quarter of the population of Canadian Muslims, those coming from South Asian countries such as India, Pakistan, and Sri Lanka make up one-fifth. Another one-fifth comes from various African countries (almost half from East Africa). The lack of appreciation for this regional diversity has turned its description into a task for many Muslim scholars (see, for instance, Mansur 2009).

Not surprisingly, therefore, many scholars who study Muslims in Canada have made it a goal to convey this internal diversity (Bakht 2008b; Esposito and Mogahed 2007; McGown 1999; Moghissi, Rahnema, and Goodman

(2009). In a book entitled *Belonging and Banishment*, for instance, Natasha Bakht (2008b, v) argues that one of her intentions is "to represent, in a thoughtful and nuanced manner, the diversity of Muslims in Canada." She points out that the contributors to this book "confirm that diversities amongst Muslims are pronounced and worthy of serious acknowledgment and celebration" (ibid.). The lack of awareness of this diversity sometimes leads to gross generalizations that do little to help clarify the issues involving Muslims.

This enormous diversity in the national origins of Canadian Muslims has generated an interesting and nuanced fact: the version of Islam practised by immigrants from different nations is a mixture of Islamic principles and the culture of the particular country from which these people have come. As well, Muslim immigrants coming from a particular country have been exposed to the political issues in their own country, which may be entirely different from those in other Muslim countries. For example, the issue of the Middle East conflict between Palestinians and Israelis has much more prominence in the psyche of Muslims coming from Arab countries than it has, for instance, in that of those coming from an Eastern Asian country like Indonesia. As well, the concerns and sensibilities of Bosnian Muslims, as a minority who lived in the secular environment of the former Yugoslavia, are very different from those from a Muslim-majority and highly religious country such as Egypt. Non-Muslim Canadians are only beginning to appreciate such differences.

Misunderstood Relationship between Islam and Muslims
The poor awareness of the demographic diversity of Canadian Muslims is supplemented by the equally poor awareness of Muslims' lived experiences, particularly in relation to what Islam means to its practitioners. The absence of Muslim voices with regard to this area has left much room for general speculation, and this has resulted in images and definitions, and debates and controversies, to which ordinary Muslims cannot easily relate.

As is the case with any other faith, the question of what Islam means to a Muslim generates many different answers, perhaps as many answers as there are Muslims. As a cognitive, emotional, intellectual, and spiritual matter, one's faith is meaningful only when it matches one's overall life profile. True, the contents of a faith are shaped historically and recorded in standard scripts; however, all those historical facts and standard themes become personalized when someone adopts them. In other words, the faithful are not passive recipients of the faith but, rather, active contributors to it.

We can see enormous variation among Muslims in terms of how they view and practise their faith: some view it as a spiritual guide, some as a manual for day-to-day practices, and some as a political manifesto. Within each of these categories, again, there are variations among individuals with regard to which elements are adopted or dropped, actively followed or left on the margins, accepted with alacrity or with hesitation, wholeheartedly believed in or only practised. Learning what Islam means to a particular Muslim, therefore, requires a conversation with that person, without any a priori assumption that "Muslimness" means only one thing.

Consider, for example, the perceived tension between the Muslim faith (or any faith, for that matter) and science. The argument commonly raised by atheists is that adherence to a faith requires blind acceptance of certain ideas, while commitment to science requires the acceptance of the superiority of reason, rational thinking, and evidence. Due to these fundamental differences, the argument goes, there is an inherent tension between Islamic faith and scientific thinking. For this reason, there is no possibility of combining the two. But the lived experiences of Muslims show that such a combination *is* possible.

Rejecting this tension between the commitment to a faith and the commitment to science, Arif Babul (2008), an astrophysicist and a devout Muslim, articulates the process through which he has managed to reconcile his devotion to his Islamic faith and his scientific career. The process, he argues, involves reinterpreting Islamic concepts and principles in such a way as to form an easy association between faith and science. While a philosopher may take issue with whether or not this is logically possible, the fact that it happens shows us that there is a process whereby a Muslim can be both devout and a scientist. One may argue that such a process creates new intellectual conflicts and/or tensions. This may be correct, but the fact is that Muslims experience and try to solve such tensions every day. And, if they are unable to resolve them, they learn to live with them. Indeed, one may end up partitioning one's mind, which, though not desirable, is certainly possible.

The ability to be committed both to faith and to science needs to be borne in mind not only by non-Muslims but also by Muslims. Quite often, Muslim leaders and clerics propose a singular image of what a Muslim should look like – in his/her beliefs, practices, appearance, and so on – and feel comfortable rejecting anyone who deviates from that image as non-Muslim or, at best, as an inauthentic Muslim. The end result is that someone who finds him/herself standing somewhere between the mainstream

Muslim population and the mainstream non-Muslim population is quite often pushed into the latter camp.

The possible mismatch between the lived experiences of Muslims and the standard/formal interpretations of Islam is well illustrated in the misgivings that some Muslims express towards the religious authorities in their communities. Using focus groups and interviews with Muslims, Karim (2008) documents an interesting development in this regard, a process that involves Muslim Canadians rethinking the concept of Islamic authority and their expectations of their religious leaders. According to Karim, Canadian Muslims are increasingly expecting their leaders "to have knowledge of Western societies, to be engaged in a practical way with their communities, and to adopt critical approaches to the understanding of Islamic tradition" (82). Karim also reports that some focus group participants expressed an interest in "critical approaches to understanding Muslim history and theology" (92). This is an extremely interesting and important development, and it is quite often lost in the highly sensationalized and extremely politicized debates about Muslims.

One result of this dual misperception – by the broader society and by the Muslim community – is that a Muslim may often find him/herself simultaneously in battle with two parties, both of which are trying to define his/her Muslimness for him/her. The existence of such a challenge is being increasingly recognized among Muslim thinkers, and the result has been attempts to theorize the lived experiences of Muslims who live in non-Muslim societies. Some of the works cited in Chapter 3 (e.g., Tariq Ramadan's notion of "Western Muslims" and al-Gharzawi's notion of "jurisprudence of the Muslim minorities") are examples of some first steps towards treating the differences between Muslims living in Muslim-majority countries and those living in non-Muslim countries as natural and unproblematic.

A Gendered Experience

Nowhere are the misunderstandings about Muslims' lived experiences more pronounced than in the case of Muslim women. Quite often, non-Muslims perceive Muslim women as submissive subjects weighed down by long histories of patriarchal Muslim societies and cultures (Khan 2008). The Islamic dress code for women (the *hijab*, marked by things such as headscarf, burka, and loose gown) is often understood by non-Muslims as a visible marker of the fact that Muslim women have internalized and submitted to those patriarchal forces. If one views the hijab in this way, one does not feel any need to ask a Muslim woman why she has chosen to wear it and what it means to her for the simple reason that one perceives her as a docile subject upon whom this garb has been forced. Observant Muslim women often find themselves between a rock and a hard place when they try to counter this simplistic image.

Muslim women may find themselves in an equally difficult position within Muslim communities when it comes to the issue of the hijab. This is a lived experience that is not shared by Muslim men. While Islamic teachings are often quoted as suggesting Muslim men should also dress modestly, there are no standard external markers for this dress – at least not to the extent that there are for Muslim women. The wearing of the hijab renders a Muslim woman clearly visible but, more important, at least in the eyes of non-Muslims, it renders her faith her master identity. On the other hand, if a Muslim woman does not wear the hijab, this creates questions in the minds of both Muslims and non-Muslims regarding how she reconciles her faith with not observing the Islamic dress code. Muslim women, therefore, find themselves feeling they owe explanations – either about why they are wearing such a "clear symbol of patriarchal oppression" or about why they are not. In other words, the perspectives that lead to personal choices made by Muslim women are often lost in translation.

The hijab-related challenges that Muslim women face are not limited to the theological justification of the personal choices they have made: they also extend to their socio-economic experiences. As is indicated in a study by Persad and Lukas (2002), Muslim women who choose to wear the hijab often find themselves easy targets for discrimination in the job market and in work environments. The tremendous pressures they face in this regard – emotionally, socially, and economically – sometimes force them to remove their hijab. This is not an easy choice, and it often comes with a great degree of emotional suffering as it could well make her feel that she is doing away with an important element of her faith. Making such a change requires one to remap one's entire faith, to rethink what is and is not essential to being a Muslim. It involves assessing how to respond to questions from both in- and out-group members, and, sometimes, it even involves a redrawing of one's social network.

The challenge gets exponentially greater when it is compounded with other disadvantages, such as being of a racial minority or struggling with a physical disability. But, even in these cases, Muslim women are actively involved in claiming their deserved place in various social spaces, as is eloquently reported in Parin Dossa's (2009) study of Muslim women of African and Iranian backgrounds who also struggle with disability. What is evident in the stories of these women is that their tireless efforts to make themselves count provides a contrast to the images of submissive Muslim women that are often held by the larger public.

The above complexities in the lives of Muslim women point to the inadequacy of those debates and discussions about Muslims that are based on highly abstract concepts, whether held by non-Muslims or the Muslim communities themselves. In a detailed and diligent review of the dominant discourses related to Muslims in Canada, Razack (2008) convincingly shows how such blind spots have misguided even the most sincere attempts by Western feminists to help Muslim women. Her central argument is that, due to such misunderstandings, some feminist activists have helped to reproduce colonial discourses that, in the end, are hurting Muslim women rather than helping them. Framing their attempts as efforts to free Muslim women from their own cultures and communities, Western feminist activists, according to Razack, impose on Muslim women a gendered identity and Western cultural norms, thus ignoring a great deal of human rights advocacy that these same Western feminists have undertaken on behalf of Muslim women. The end result, naturally, has been that many Muslim women cannot relate to the efforts of their Western feminist sisters.

Misrepresentation in the Media

Inaccurate media images exist about almost any group. But what makes this a particularly important issue in the case of Muslims living in Western countries is the relative ease with which those images find their way into powerful popular media. The amount of media coverage they receive is another distinct feature of the lives of Canadian Muslims.

The impact of media content on the lives of Muslims is better appreciated when it is seen against the background of the reasons for Muslim immigration and the features of Canadian society that Muslims most enjoy. In response to a question in the LSIC, a large proportion of Muslims cite the peacefulness of Canada's social and political environment as the feature they like most about this country. This is to be expected, given the lack of such peacefulness in many of the countries from which these immigrants have come. Disseminating the results of a focus group study, Leuprecht and Winn (2011) report that the participants view as desirable the "ability to lead a quiet life." This ability, however, can be hard to achieve when one finds one's faith community and identity constantly under discussion (mostly in a negative way), as is clear from the following statements from two focus group participants: "If another person commits a crime, we do not hear about his religion first. But when it is a Muslim, you do." And: "All Muslims are not the monster created by the propaganda machine" (both quoted in Leuprecht and Winn 2011, 21).

The media's unusually extensive coverage of issues related to Muslims has played a major role in shaping the relationship between Muslims and non-Muslims in Canada. One example of this surfaced during the so-called reasonable accommodation controversy in Quebec in 2007. The thorough report of this controversy, generated by prominent scholars Lucien Bouchard and Charles Taylor (2008), clearly points to the role played by the media and the degree to which there was a mismatch between the facts and media reports. Another example is the controversy surrounding the issue of Sharia law in Ontario back in 2005-06. At the heart of this controversy was the question of whether or not Muslims should be allowed to settle such domestic issues as family disputes and inheritance in a special tribunal that would operate according to Islamic principles. The controversy finally ended when the Arbitration Act was abolished after having been in place for fifteen years. The distinct place of Muslims in the media coverage could be seen in the fact that, during all fifteen years that this act had been enjoyed by Christians and Jews, it never received the kind of coverage that it did once Muslims began using it (Siddiqui 2008).

A more recent example of the special attention that Muslims receive in Canadian media surfaced in Calgary in 2010, after the election of Canada's first Muslim mayor (Wingrove 2010). A major item in the debates that surfaced after Naheed Nenshi's victory was his Muslim background, and that someone with this religious background could be elected as mayor in a city and province known for its political conservatism. The constant reassurances by the mayor-elect that the city's residents voted for his platform, without regard to his religious background, did little to mitigate what a surprise this was to many across the country.

In response to what a great number of Muslims consider imbalanced and biased coverage in the media, many Muslim organizations have emerged to provide an antidote and to represent Canadian Muslims more generally. Some of the more active and visible of these organizations are: the Canadian Islamic Congress, the Muslim Canadian Congress, the Muslim Association of Canada, the Ahmadiyya Muslim Community Canada, and the Canadian Muslim Union. The connection between these organizations and ordinary Muslims reveals another interesting anomaly. In their focus group study of Canadian Muslims, Leuprecht and Winn (2011) report that, to their surprise, despite the participants' high levels of interest in politics, they never mention anything about Muslim political advocacy groups and organizations. Indeed, many, did not know anything about these organizations. To an outsider, this may sound quite curious. But it makes sense when put within the context of the internal diversity of Muslim communities addressed earlier. This diversity relates to national origin, culture, political issues, immigrant class, language, and the branch of Islam to which one belongs. And it makes it extremely difficult for Muslim organizations to remain relevant to their membership for a long period of time. Canadian geography only adds to this problem as it ensures that the Muslim population is spread across vast distances. In an environment like this, the more popular and successful advocacy groups tend to be those that are smaller, locally based, and more homogeneous (as opposed to large umbrella organizations).

The high visibility of Muslim organizations, combined with the low level of Muslims' engagement with them, creates another gap in the public perception of Muslims in Canada: the public often equates the positions taken in the mass media by the leaders of these organizations with what all Muslims think. While in many cases such leaders may indeed be in touch with their constituencies, in other cases a low level of grassroots engagement may create a gap between the views of rank-and-file Muslims and those of their spokespersons. One implication of this potential gap is that the extremist (or moderate) voices of some Muslim leaders may not necessarily reflect the sentiments of ordinary Muslims. By extension, if efforts to reach out to Muslims are only directed at Muslim advocacy groups, they may do little to impress the body of the Canadian Muslim population.

The potential gap between Canadian Muslims and Muslim advocacy groups has implications for research. A thorough understanding of Canadian Muslims requires us to go beyond the Muslim voices in the media to where we find the bulk of the Muslim population. Ignoring the distinction between Muslim media voices and the Muslim population has posed serious problems for many studies of Muslims. In trying to find subjects for interviews, for instance, some researchers rely heavily on Islamic organizations to suggest names and to provide contacts. Those organizations, in turn, may take a long time to respond, making sure that the names put forward will present a good image of the faith, the organization, and the larger

Muslim community. The end result of a process like this is a politically correct image that may or may not reflect the realities of the lives of Canadian Muslims.

The various dimensions of diversity within the Canadian Muslim population have just started to find their way into the thinking of non-Muslim Canadians. As a result of the studies conducted by academics and the activities organized by community organizations, the popular views on Muslims are moving away from stereotypical images and towards more realistic accounts. However, the change is very slow, and it is certainly not amounting to "a revolution in our understanding of Muslim populations in the West," as is claimed by Saunders (2012a). The currents of misunderstanding regarding Muslims issues run too deep to be quickly corrected by the simple addition of more information about Muslims. There are grand narratives at work, and these slant the ways in which people make sense of even "unbiased" pieces of information. As a result, many studies of Muslims rightly aim at analyzing those grand narratives.

Grand Narratives at Work

In his book *Islamic Peril*, Karim (2003) argues that the dominant discourses in the Western media portray Muslims as the "Other," the enemy, in response to whom a nation-building project can be carried out. This, according to him, was to fill the vacuum created by the collapse of the communist block and the end of the Cold War in the late 1980s and early 1990s. Karim argues that, with some exceptions (such as Robert Fisk), individual journalists tend to use this narrative as their analytical framework, without questioning its validity or showing any desire to critique it. Karim's book was well received at the time of its publication in 2000, but it was deemed even more relevant after the events of 9/11 and the intensification of the media's coverage on Muslims, which resulted in its republication in 2003.

Searching for other grand narratives in the media, Jasmin Jiwani (2006) points to the presence of a structure based on racial inequality, which has created a context within which Muslim issues are understood and discussed. Such a structure, according to Jiwani, is present in the case of all people of colour, including non-Muslim South Asians and Aboriginal peoples. Jiwani does not go as far as Karim, who links such structures to broader historical forces such as nation-building projects, but she does make a case for how the seemingly random pieces of media coverage could be linked to, and are influenced by, a less visible narrative aimed at sustaining a particular structure of inequality in Canada.

Using a variety of international and Canadian case studies, Razack (2008) convincingly shows that such grand narratives about Muslims have to do with Western empire building. Utilizing concepts such as "race thinking" and "camps," she argues that the popular perceptions of Muslims as well as their treatment in the West fit perfectly into this broader narrative, which tends to establish or recreate a hierarchical "structure of citizenship." In such a structure, certain groups are assigned a permanent lower status and are perceived to be outside the realms of citizenship and rule of law. As a result, they are treated as "rightless." Those groups are then assigned to camps – a part of the social space to which normal laws and rights do not apply. Extreme examples include Nazi Germany's Holocaust, Soviet Russia's gulags, and the United States's Guantanamo. While Muslims are not the only subjects of those powerful forces, they are the most recent ones.

According to Razack (2008), in the case of Muslims, the above narrative has been formed around two images: "dangerous" Muslim men and "imperilled" Muslim women. Both groups are viewed, in the discourses informed by the empire-building narrative, as being trapped in the premodern era – Muslim men because of their patriarchal and violence-prone tendencies, and Muslim women because of their docility and internalization of patriarchal culture. This narrative suggests that there is a need for "modern forces" to intervene to fix the problem by keeping Muslim men in check and freeing Muslim women from their yoke. In her immensely rich case studies, Razack shows how these two misguided images of Muslim men and women manifest themselves in the imprisonment of Muslim men in Canada and the restriction of their rights to due process, in the torture of Iraqi men in Abu-Ghraib, in the treatment of Muslim women in Norway, and in the Sharia debate in Canada.

As Razack argues, such images have influenced not only uninformed and insensitive minds but also (surprisingly) the thinking of many Western feminists. Their efforts to promote gender equality and to protect "Muslim women from their violent communities" have turned into campaigns to "deculturalize" Muslims and to "emancipate" Muslim women from their communities and from their religion. This misguided vision, which greatly influenced the so-called Sharia debates in Ontario, ignored religious women of Muslim backgrounds almost entirely (Bakht 2007) and also provided justification for empire-building campaigns such as "the war on terror" (Razack 2008).

Many female Muslim scholars and activists in Canada have taken on the task of debunking this image of the imperilled Muslim woman and the misunderstandings surrounding it. In an analysis of recent Canadian debates regarding prohibiting Muslim women from wearing headscarves, or *niqab*, in sporting events (e.g., soccer and taekwondo) and in certain professions (e.g., prison guards), along with the need to remove their face covering in election polls and on buses, Bakht (2008a) notes that the stereotypical image of Muslim women as imperilled seems now to be joined by an image of Muslim women as dangerous – something previously reserved for Muslim men. She argues that one result of this has been that Canadians' perception of Muslim women is now oscillating between that of victim and that of aggressor – a group that should be both protected and protected against.

The need to pay attention to, and to debunk, such grand narratives stems from the fact that they have the potential to negatively influence even well-intentioned efforts to ameliorate the challenges faced by Muslims. Hirji (2011) shows the existence of such influences in a study of the contents of three TV shows – *24*, *Lost*, and *Little Mosque on the Prairie* – that tried to compensate for the underrepresentation of Muslims in the entertainment world. According to Hirji, despite their noble motive, these shows contain the same negative elements that are found elsewhere. She argues that, in some cases, these shows may have even served "to reinforce misunderstanding about Islam and gender, rather than challenging it" (44). If nothing else, studies of this kind show the complexity and the multifaceted nature of the problem at hand, and the need for a multidimensional response to it.

Power of the Media

This chapter sketches some of the major areas of misperception and misrepresentation with regard to the lives of Canadian Muslims. The power of the media in this process cannot be overemphasized as its effect does not remain on TV screens or in movie theatres; rather, it influences people's thinking and behaviours. Such influence is especially acute when a particular image is repeatedly delivered through various media and in different forums. As Hirji (2011, 37) puts it: "While the average viewer may be able to distinguish between fact and fiction, this becomes increasingly difficult if a variety of media come together to create a consistent picture." The repetition and omnipresence of an image creates what Peter Berger (1967) calls "plausibility structures" – social processes that legitimize certain practices, ideas, or beliefs – as a result of which a particular view becomes readily accepted.

That said, we should also be aware of the limitations of an exclusive focus on mass media. First, such studies are mostly based on the qualitative and in-depth analysis – or what Geertz (1973) called "thick description" – of media contents. While very good at showing the subtle details of media contents, such studies are eminently vulnerable to the possibility of reading too much into them. Second, one must be careful not to take extracted images for reality. It is one thing to show that media present certain images about a particular issue; it is quite another to show the extent to which such images have actually shaped the ways in which people think and behave in their daily lives. In other words, showing that a particular image is constantly reinforced in the media and has great potential to influence people's thoughts and behaviours is not the same as showing that this potential has been actualized.

This last point is part of a greater debate and a more fundamental question in the field of media research: To what extent does the media influence, as opposed to reflect, public opinion? What is certain is that the contents of media products such as TV shows and films reflect the attitudes and opinions of their producers, not necessarily of their consumers. Even if a show is particularly popular, this cannot be understood to indicate that all of its messages and images are accepted. One would need to determine that something is popular *because of* those images rather than *in spite of* them.

There are several reasons that a particular media image may fail to enter people's daily lives. One of these could be the poor quality of its mode of delivery. A recent example of this is the movie *The Innocence of Muslims*, which created such a violent and bloody uproar in the Muslim world. As many observers noted, if such a strong wave of protest had not occurred, this film would have received very little attention, mostly due to its extremely poor quality. A poorly delivered message is like a bad translation, resulting in the meaning – in this case, the negative images – being lost in the process.

Something else that could undermine the influence of the mainstream media is the presence of alternative and social media. Through the social and political movements of recent years we have learned that social media can effectively counter the influences of mainstream media (e.g., TV, cinema, and print media). The most recent examples of this occurred during the 2008 presidential election in the United States and the recent uprising in the Middle East known as the Arab Spring. Both of these examples show that an exclusive reliance on an analysis of mainstream media conveys only part of the picture. It is necessary to go beyond media images into the realm of people's behaviours and attitudes.

This need is the point of departure for the findings presented in the next chapter, in which I examine the overall status of Canadian Muslims with regard to several indicators of attachment and belonging to Canada as well as with regard to measures of integration into Canadian society. The reported data are mostly comparative, showing the differences between Muslims living in Canada and some other countries, between Canadian Muslims and non-Muslims, and between the situations in Quebec and the rest of Canada.

7

The Muslim Question in Canada

────────── Is There One?

Even a cursory look at the global news involving Muslim immigrants shows that Canada is in a class by itself: many alarming signs that have surfaced in other countries are clearly absent in Canada. The country has not witnessed any Muslim terrorist activities comparable to the 9/11 events in the United States, the subway bombings in London, the assassination of filmmaker Theo van Gogh in the Netherlands, and the railway explosions in Madrid (the only activities of note were two thwarted terrorist plots in 2006 and 2013, known as the "Toronto 18" and the "Via Rail" plots, respectively, and resulting in the arrest of eighteen and two suspects, respectively). Nor did Canada witness the kind of outpouring of Muslim anger that occurred worldwide in response to such events as protests against Salman Rushdie's *The Satanic Verses*, the publication of the Danish cartoons of Prophet Muhammad, and, recently, the screening of the movie *The Innocence of Muslims*. These differences signal the possibility that Canada's context differs from those of other countries with sizable Muslim immigrant populations.

This difference is visible not only through a casual reading of the world news but also in various comparative studies between Canada and other countries. In a study of Somali Muslims in Toronto and London (England), for instance, McGown (1999) convincingly shows the visibly different experiences of these two communities, with a much more accepting and welcoming environment in Canada than in England. Other studies corroborate this finding (see, for instance, Moghissi 2003, 2009; Moghissi, Rahnema, and Goodman 2009). This difference, with regard not only to Muslims but also to other immigrants, has resulted in a scholarly discussion of what could be called "Canadian exceptionalism" (see, for instance, Banting and Kymlicka 2004; Kazemipur 2006, 2009; Kymlicka 2009; Kymlicka and Banting 2006; TVO 2011). This must be music to the ears of Canadian policy makers, who, in the words of Jason Kenney, Canada's minister (2008-13) of citizenship, immigration, and multiculturalism, like "to avoid the kind of ethnic enclaves or parallel communities that exist in some European countries" (quoted in Orwin 2009).

Despite the general validity of the notion of Canadian exceptionalism, a closer and more systematic examination reveals some not-so-rosy elements that are signs of potential or actual trouble beneath the surface. One such sign surfaced in the mid-1990s during the controversies surrounding the issue of Sharia law in Ontario, the most populous of Canada's provinces. According to the Arbitration Act, the Muslim community in Ontario was allowed to use Sharia law to process certain civic problems based on principles respected by Muslims and to do so in a court outside the Canadian justice system. Despite the completely voluntary nature of this court system and the Arbitration Act's fifteen-year-old precedent, opposition was so extreme that the result was not only the abolition of Sharia Law but also of the Act itself, which had allowed for such practices for other faith communities.

About a decade later, in the mid-2000s, a similar controversy surfaced, this time in Quebec, the second most populous province in Canada. The controversy was over the issue of "reasonable accommodation" and the extent to which such accommodation should be granted to religious and cultural minorities in the province. While this issue was not exclusively focused on Muslims, and included other minorities such as Jews and Sikhs, the majority of the controversial cases involved Muslims. At the heart of this issue was a deep concern on the part of the native-born population that accommodating immigrants and minorities, particularly Muslims, might lead to the loss of crucial elements of the distinct Quebecois identity – that is, the French language, a secular system, and a gender-egalitarian social structure. The inter-ethnic frictions in Quebec that emerged later on led to the formation of the Bouchard-Taylor Commission and the subsequent publication of an elaborate report (Bouchard and Taylor 2008), which thoroughly documents all aspects of this conflict.

The underlying sentiments in the Quebec case were revealed through the declaration of the so-called Herouxville Town Charter, which was signed by six municipalities (Municipalité-Hérouxville 2010). The document was meant to codify what it calls the "social life and habits and customs of all residents" of those municipalities in order to inform potential newcomers of the lifestyles and behaviours expected of them. While the document did not specifically mention anything about immigrants, one clause indicates that they were the target audience of this charter: "We would especially like to inform the new arrivals that the lifestyle that they left behind in their birth country cannot be brought here with them and they would have to adapt to their new social identity."

Although the document does not mention Muslims, the discussion of some of the practices that were perceived to be dominant in Muslim societies shows that the charter was particularly directed at them. For example, with regard to women, the charter says:

> We consider that men and women are of the same value. Having said this, we consider that a woman can drive a car, vote, sign checks, dance, decide for herself, speak her peace, dress as she sees fit respecting of course the democratic decency, walk alone in public places, study, have a job, have her own belongings and anything else that a man can do. These are our standards and our way of life. However, we consider that killing women in public beatings, or burning them alive are not part of our standards of life.

The same message was conveyed in another paragraph in the charter, which states: "We listen to music, we drink alcoholic beverages in public or private places, we dance and at the end of every year we decorate a tree with balls and tinsel and some lights. This is normally called 'Christmas Decorations' or also 'Christmas Tree' letting us rejoice in the notion of our national heritage and not necessarily a religious holiday. These festivities are authorized in public, schools, and institutions and also in private." With regard to health care, the document states: "There is no law voted democratically that prohibits a woman treating a man and a man treating a woman." These and many other references confirm that the fault line is not between the local population and immigrants per se; rather, it is between the local population and Muslim immigrants.

The Sharia law debate in Ontario and the reasonable accommodation controversy in Quebec are just two very visible cases that point to the possibility of a tense relationship between Muslim immigrants and native-born Canadians. On the other hand, the relative calmness that followed those heated debates may suggest that, whatever the sources of the tensions, they are now resolved. The difficulty with such statements is that they rely heavily on media reports rather than on what is happening on the ground. Given the unreliability of media representation with regard to this, it would be prudent to examine the situation using more comprehensive and systematically gathered data. This is the task of the following chapters.

Starting with this chapter, using data from several nation-wide Canadian surveys, I examine the place of Muslims in Canadian society and the relationship between them and the native-born population. I also explore various dimensions of Muslim attachment to Canada. I present the data under three categories: (1) Muslims in Canada, (2) Muslim and non-Muslim immigrants, and (3) the future of Muslims in Canada. I conclude with a comparison between Quebec and the rest of Canada.

Muslims in Canada: Is There a Canadian Exceptionalism?

Before getting into inter-group relations, it might be useful to get a general sense of how Muslims feel about their lives in Canada as a whole. Figure 7.1 reports Canadian Muslims' responses to three very broad indicators of their overall situation in this country. The bar on the left shows the distribution of the responses to the question regarding whether the respondent is satisfied with the way things are going in Canada, which indicates that about 80 percent of Muslims have given a positive response. This is an incredibly high

FIGURE 7.1
Overall indicators of satisfaction, Muslim Canadians

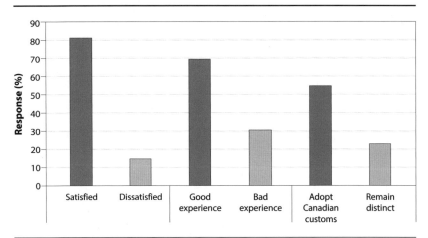

Source: Environics Institute, Survey of Canadian Muslims, 2006.

number and is close to the numbers reported by the native-born population. The middle bar in Figure 7.1 reports Muslim immigrants' responses to a related measure: whether they have experienced anything negative that might have been related to their race, ethnicity, or religion. Here again, a very high proportion (70 percent) of Muslims report having had only good experiences. The high proportion of satisfied Muslims and those with good experiences is probably a decent reflection of the differences in the experiences of Muslims in Canada as opposed to those in other countries with sizable Muslim minority populations.

Figure 7.1 also reports Muslims' answers to another closely related and crucial question: To what degree are they willing to adopt Canadian cultural customs rather than keeping their cultural identity distinct from that of Canadians? The data are reported for the two extreme answers and show that more than half of Canadian Muslims are willing to adopt Canadian customs, with about one-quarter of them wanting to remain distinct. Although not reflected in the graph, another one-quarter seems to believe that they could combine the two options. If we interpret this middle answer as being open to adopting Canadian customs, then about three-quarters of Muslims see no problem in adopting Canadian cultural customs – a figure that is very close to those reported for the two previous indicators of satisfaction and good experience.

It would be interesting to compare these numbers with those reported by Muslims in the United States. Responding to a similar question in a survey conducted around the same time (Pew Research Center 2007), 43 percent of American Muslims indicated their willingness to adopt American customs – about 10 percent lower than the Canadian numbers. A breakdown of these answers shows a lower-than-average score for native-born Muslims and a higher-than-average score for foreign-born (immigrant) Muslims. Among the latter, the highest rate is reported by those who arrived in the United States before 1990, with a percentage (55 percent) that, interestingly, is identical to that of Canadian Muslims. In other words, the average score for the proportion of Canadian Muslims willing to adopt Canadian customs is equivalent to the number reported for the most-willing segment of the Muslim population in the United States.

The above data, however, talk about the feelings of Muslims towards Canada, not towards Canadians. The distinction between these two concepts is important because they refer to two different societal dimensions into which immigrants and/or minorities could integrate: the institutional and the communal. The institutional refers more to the way in which the law

FIGURE 7.2
Native-born Canadians' views on Islam

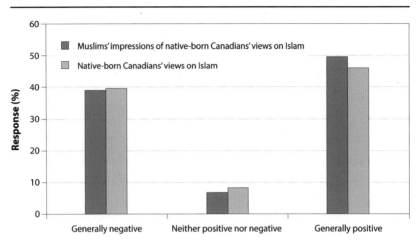

Source: Environics Institute, Survey of Canadian Muslims, 2006.

and public institutions function, while the communal refers more to the way people behave. These two dimensions are very different, so it is important to examine both.

There are several indicators that can act as thermometers for inter-group feelings – in this case Muslim and native-born Canadians. One such indicator is Muslims' impression of how native-born Canadians feel towards Islam; a closely related indicator is how native-born Canadians actually *do* feel towards Islam. Figure 7.2 reports both these indicators, and, interestingly enough, the two are almost identical. This similarity in reported responses may be taken as a sign that the perceptions of Muslims regarding how they are viewed by those around them are quite accurate. In the following pages, we see more examples of such similarities.

The distribution of native-born Canadians' views on Islam shows an almost perfect bipolar structure, with about 40 percent having a generally negative view, 45 percent having a generally positive view, and less than 10 percent feeling ambivalent. In trying to extract the implications of this particular pattern, one should keep two important points in mind. First, in the absence of any other sources of information, views on Islam are heavily shaped by the contents of the popular media; and, as I have discussed, in recent years media content has been full of negative images of Islam and Muslims. Second, a negative view of Islam on the part of a native-born

Canadian does not automatically translate into a negative view of Muslims. While the former can certainly influence the latter, imagining an effect in the opposite direction is equally plausible; that is, a positive view of Muslims could result in the development of a more positive view of Islam. While a view of Islam tends to reflect a philosophical position, a view of Muslims tends to reflect social realities and experiences (e.g., meeting a Muslim). Given this, it is important to supplement views on Islam (a philosophical position) with views on Muslims (a social position).

Figures 7.3 and 7.4 speak more directly to the social aspect of the relationship between Canadian Muslims and native-born Canadians. Responding to a question regarding what proportion of Canadians hold hostile views of Muslims, the overwhelming majority (about three-quarters) of Muslim respondents indicated that very few or just some have such opinions; the number who think otherwise is less than one-fifth. This confirms the distinction suggested above, that the negative view Canadians have towards Islam does not necessarily result in the development of hostile views towards Muslims. This is a healthy sign, and it is supplemented by an equally healthy sign from Muslims. When asked about how favourably they view Christians – a proxy for non-immigrant Canadians – about 80 percent of Canadian Muslims reported that they had either somewhat favourable or very favourable opinions of them, with less than 10 percent having somewhat unfavourable and very unfavourable opinions. The answers to a similar

FIGURE 7.3

Muslims: In your opinion, how many Canadians are hostile towards Muslims?

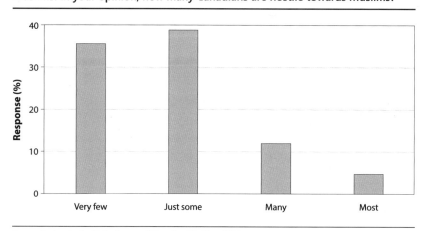

Source: Environics Institute, Survey of Canadian Muslims, 2006.

FIGURE 7.4

Muslims: Would you say you have a very/somewhat favourable/unfavourable opinion of Christians?

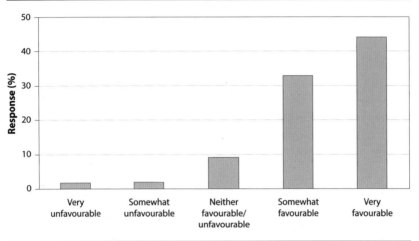

Note: Environics Institute, Survey of Canadian Muslims, 2006.

question on Jews generate a similar pattern, although, compared to Christians, the percentage is lower for favourable and higher for unfavourable (around 50 and 20 percent, respectively). The combined patterns of the responses to these two questions point to a reasonably healthy inter-group environment.

In light of this reasonably healthy state of inter-group attitudes, the negative impressions of Islam among about half of Canadians, and the ability of Muslims to accurately sense those impressions, should not be a cause for concern. After all, an overwhelming majority of Muslims seem to acknowledge that while those negative views about Islam exist, they have not generated much hostility towards Muslims. Perhaps as a reaction to this, Muslims have not developed negative feelings towards Christians and/or Jews. In a sense, this may imply that both native-born Canadians and Canadian Muslims have managed to make a distinction between the attitudinal aspects and the behaviourial aspects of inter-group relations. This is a very important distinction and is one to which I return in later chapters.

The data presented so far in the chapter may be taken, not unreasonably, to imply that Muslims should have no major concern about their lives in Canada. After all, they have had mostly good experiences, are satisfied, have favourable views of their Christian and Jewish fellow citizens, do not feel much hostility coming their way from the larger population, and, perhaps as a consequence, feel comfortable with being a part of Canadian society and adopting the customs of their new home. The status of the relationship between Muslims and Canada is definitely different from that between Muslims and other immigrant-receiving countries – something that may be taken as an indirect confirmation of the presence of some kind of Canadian exceptionalism.

This is true, but it is not the whole truth. As mentioned in previous chapters, the current debates on the issue of Muslim minorities revolve not only around the assumption that there are problems with Muslims integrating into host countries but also around the assumption that Muslims' experiences in this regard are unlike those of all other immigrant groups. The latter point has been the thrust of what we call Muslim exceptionalism – the belief that Muslims face challenges that are different from those faced by all other groups, either in quality or in quantity. To address this issue, we need to compare Muslim and non-Muslim immigrants to Canada in terms of the various indicators of their attachment to the country.

Muslim and Non-Muslim Immigrants: Is There a Muslim Exceptionalism?

One broad indicator of an individual's or a group's attachment to a society is the level of trust shown towards the general population. Figure 7.5 reports the percentage of people of different religious backgrounds who have expressed their trust in their fellow citizens. Muslims are the second lowest among all groups, led only by Jehovah's Witnesses, but they are the very last among immigrant groups. While this pattern is based on the Canadian General Social Survey conducted in 2003, the data from other surveys conducted at different times – such as the Ethnic Diversity Survey conducted in 2005 – show a more or less similar pattern, which speaks to the relative robustness of the emerged pattern.

To some, a question on trust addressed to the general population may appear to be too abstract to reveal anything concrete about the respondents. They may argue that the lack of knowledge about whom the respondents have in mind as "others" makes it difficult to judge the respondents' true connection to their society. This concern has resulted in the inclusion of some additional measures of trust in various surveys in which specific target populations (such as neighbours, co-workers, and classmates) are mentioned.

FIGURE 7.5

Proportion of population who think "most people can be trusted," by religion

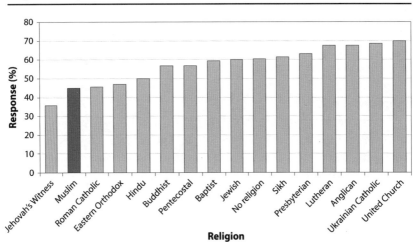

Source: Statistics Canada, Canadian General Social Survey, 2003 (cycle 17).

Among these, trust in neighbours is particularly important as the neighbour-hood is an area of social space in which, unlike workplace or educational environments, there is the least amount of competition and the highest like-lihood of sharing a common cause.

Figure 7.6 shows the results of a question on trust in neighbours, and it indicates the percentage of people of different religious backgrounds who have chosen a score of 4 or 5 on a 5-point trust Likert scale. Here again, Muslims score among the lowest (i.e., they are one of the bottom three groups among those with large immigrant populations). This, in combina-tion with the previous question on trust towards the general population, covers the whole range of social space, from the broadest and the most abstract to the narrowest and most concrete. And, at both ends, Muslims' scores are either the lowest or one of the lowest. The relative consistency of Muslims' low scores on different measures of trust, and in different surveys conducted in different times, gives us confidence that what we are seeing is not just a statistical artifact. Rather, the surveys seem to touch on something deep and stable among Muslims in their relationship with Canadian society and the population at large – something that is different from what we see in other groups.

FIGURE 7.6

Trust in neighbours (proportion who reported the highest degrees –
4/5 and 5/5), by religion, 2005

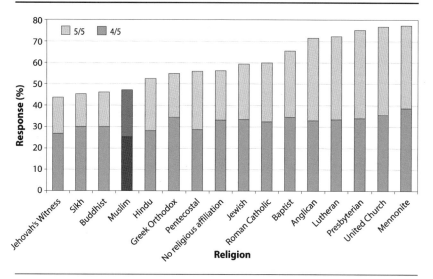

Source: Statistics Canada, Ethnic Diversity Survey, 2005.

In capturing the nature of the relationship between an individual or a group and the broader society, trust is not just one variable alongside others: it is fundamental and influences many possible ways in which one could be attached to a society. Trust is the backbone of many interactions and associational dynamics. As recent scholarship on social capital shows, the presence of trust is associated with a heavy degree of citizen engagement in politics, volunteer activities, civil projects, and crime control. As well, it contributes to the smoother functioning of economic and political systems. So a lack of trust in the general population could easily result in a lack of engagement in other areas of social life (for a discussion on social capital in Canada and the United States, see Kazemipur 2009; Putnam 2001).

One such engagement deficit can be found in the area of participation in elections. Figure 7.7 reports the proportion of the population of each faith community that voted in the last federal election. As the graph shows, here again one of the lowest rates is reported by Muslims, second only to Jehovah's Witnesses. In other words, among immigrant groups, Muslims have the lowest level of participation in the most basic and fundamental

FIGURE 7.7

Proportion of population (eligible voters) who voted in the last federal
election, by religion, 2005

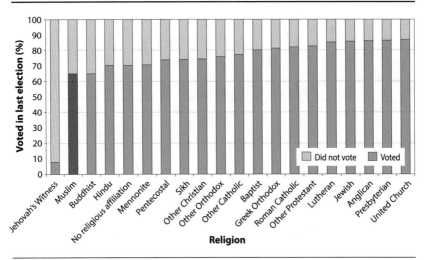

Note: Eligible voters are those who are of legal age, and who are Canadian citizens.
Source: Statistics Canada, Ethnic Diversity Survey, 2005.

type of political engagement. It should be noted that the score reported
here is for those who are eligible to vote (i.e., those with Canadian citizenship); therefore, the low scores for Muslims cannot be attributed to their
ineligibility due to immigrant status.

One factor that could promote one to engage more with the broader society is the general level of one's satisfaction with life. Figure 7.8 reports the
results for different religions. While the overall levels are quite high for all
groups – between 70 and 83 percent being very satisfied – the variations
among groups are noteworthy. Here again, Muslims report one of the lowest scores, second only to Buddhists.

A very broad but useful indicator of immigrants' attachment to their new
homes is their answer to the question regarding whether or not they would
come to the country again if they had the chance to repeat the process. The
data from the LSIC allow for a quick examination of this indicator. Remember
that LSIC data are based on long surveys of immigrants who landed in
Canada during the year 2001. Those immigrants were surveyed at three
points in time: six months, two years, and four years after their initial arrival
in Canada. The longitudinal nature of the survey, along with its decent sample size (about seventy-seven hundred respondents present in all three

FIGURE 7.8

Satisfaction with life as a whole (proportion who reported the highest degrees – 4/5 and 5/5), by religion, 2005

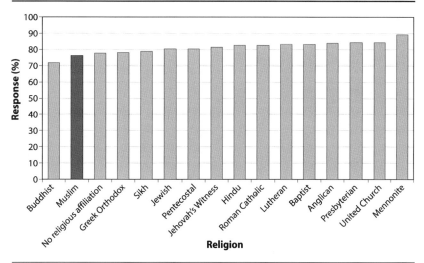

Source: Statistics Canada, Ethnic Diversity Survey, 2005.

waves), allows for an extremely rich assessment of the experiences of immigrants in the first few years of life in their new homes.

Figure 7.9 reports the answers of the immigrants of various religious backgrounds to the question regarding whether they would migrate again. The question was asked in the third wave of the survey (i.e., after the immigrants had lived in Canada for about four years). While the scores are quite high for all groups – an indication of the generally positive experiences of immigrants in Canada – when different groups are compared, Muslims are again positioned towards the bottom (i.e., the second last group, next to those of no religion).

Collectively, the data presented thus far point to two facts. First, Muslims report a relatively high level of satisfaction with, and successful integration into, Canada, especially in comparison to Muslims in other immigrant-receiving Western democracies. This distinct experience is partly a reflection of a generally pleasant social environment in Canada, what some have referred to as Canadian exceptionalism. Second, when compared to other ethnic minority and immigrant groups, Muslims score consistently low on a variety of indicators of attachment to Canada. This may loosely speak to what I call Muslim exceptionalism.

FIGURE 7.9

Mean score for the factor "would come to Canada again" (Wave 3 of LSIC data), by religion, 2005

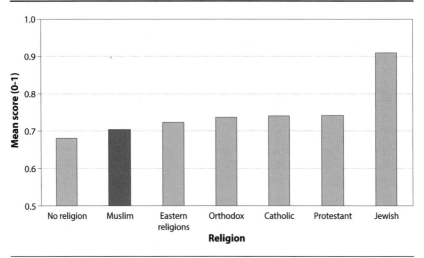

Source: Statistics Canada, Longitudinal Survey of Immigrants to Canada, 2005.

If this is the current situation, what might the future bring? Will things get better or change for the worse? Does the current healthy situation imply that we do not have to worry about the future? It is extremely hard to come up with empirically informed answers to these questions; however, there are some data that might provide us with some hints.

The Future of Muslims in Canada

The optimism about the status of Muslims in Canada reflected in the first section of this chapter is somewhat dampened by the comparisons of Muslims and non-Muslims in the second. This optimism is further weakened when we explore the direction things might take in the future.

One surprising piece of evidence for this comes from the responses of Muslims to a question regarding how concerned they are about their future in Canada. As Figure 7.10 illustrates, more than 55 percent of Muslims state that they are either somewhat worried or very worried about the future. To be sure, this should not be taken as a prediction of what is to come, but it should be taken as a clear indication of how Muslims perceive the direction of current trends. This high level of concern about the future might negatively affect the strength of Muslims' attachment to Canada.

FIGURE 7.10

Muslims: How concerned, if at all, are you about the future of Muslims in this country?

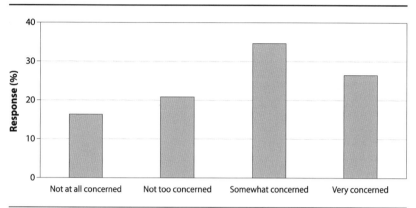

Source: Environics Institute, Survey of Canadian Muslims, 2006.

A second, though indirect, piece of evidence that seems to corroborate the above observation comes from the LSIC data. In all three waves of this survey, the immigrants who participated in it were asked to comment on their Canadian experience: Had it been the same as, better, or worse than what they had expected? In reporting the answers to this question, Figure 7.11 shows the proportion of immigrants of various religious backgrounds

FIGURE 7.11

Proportion of immigrants who think their Canadian experience has been "better than expected," by religion and time

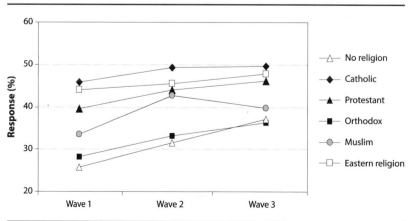

Source: Statistics Canada, Longitudinal Survey of Immigrants to Canada, 2005.

who considered their Canadian experience to be better than expected. The trend lines show a rise from one wave to another – a rise that is more pronounced for certain groups than others. Muslim immigrants are the only anomaly here: for them, the percentages start declining after their second year in Canada.

There are no data available to show how this trend continues after the fourth year. However, given the importance of immigrants' experiences in their first few years of being in Canada with regard to shaping their long-lasting perceptions of this country, it is not unreasonable to expect that the declining trend will continue even after the fourth year. One indirect indicator of this is the data cited in Figure 7.9 concerning the responses that Muslim immigrants gave to the question regarding whether they would come to Canada again, knowing what they know after having spent four years here. The fact that Muslims had the second lowest score may indicate that the decline that started in the second year would continue after the fourth year. It should be noted that the scores are generally quite high for all groups, including Muslims, but that the Muslim score is low in comparison to that of other groups. This implies that their experiences might differ from those of others.

Muslim immigrants are not just the only group for whom the percentages decline after the second year but they are also the group with the sharpest increase in the level of positive experiences within their first two years in Canada. In two short years, the proportion of Muslim immigrants whose migration experience was better than anticipated jumps ten percentage points. The combination of these two pieces of data certainly points to the existence of an immigration experience for Muslims that differs from that of other immigrants. The drastic change in the direction of this trend may also point to how things may evolve in the future, at least as far as Muslims' attachment to Canada is concerned.

The sources of Muslims' concerns about their future in Canada are not fully known. If we can assume that those concerns have their origins in the challenges that Muslims face today, then the existing data can give us some hints about them. Figure 7.12 reports the percentage of Muslims who have expressed their concerns about acts of discrimination against Muslims, the levels of unemployment among Muslims, and the rise of extremism among Muslims; the corresponding proportions are around 70, 60, and 50 percent, respectively. These are alarmingly high numbers, with significant consequences for Muslims' level of attachment to Canada.

FIGURE 7.12

Muslims: How concerned are you about the occurrence of acts of discrimination against Muslims, levels of unemployment among Muslims, and the rise of extremism among Muslims?

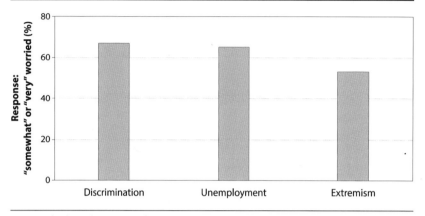

Source: Environics Institute, Survey of Canadian Muslims, 2006.

To what extent are these three concerns logically correlated with one another? In other words, could one argue that these are not three separate entities but, rather, different manifestations of the same phenomenon? And that resolving one of them – for example, unemployment – would automatically result in a similar decline in others? A comparison of Canada and the United States in this regard suggests that such a correlation cannot be assumed. In a survey conducted by the Pew Research Group (2007, 36), American Muslims were asked a related question concerning the "most important problems facing US Muslims," the responses to which show that the highest percentages are reported for things such as discrimination, racism, prejudice, being viewed as terrorists, ignorance about Islam, stereotyping, and negative media portrayals, the combined total being 67 percent. Concern about jobs and financial problems, on the other hand, appears at the bottom of the list, with only 2 percent of Muslims reporting it as the most serious problem. This odd combination and the peculiar difference between Canada the United States are worth reflecting upon.

At least on the surface, the above data seem to imply that the racism Muslims experience in the United States does not necessarily translate into fewer economic opportunities for Muslims. In Canada, discrimination and economic opportunities both seem to be equally high for Muslims. To some extent, this may be attributed to the much greater size of the American economy, which may provide more job opportunities for everyone – including Muslims. As a result, the dislike of Muslims on the part of certain segments of the American population is not associated with economic threat – at least not to the same extent as it is in Canada.

This is a hypothesis that does not easily lend itself to empirical verification. But here again, indirect support for it might be found through determining the association between (1) people's reactions to Muslims in different areas of the country and (2) the levels of economic prosperity in those areas. In Canada, a comparison between Muslims in Quebec and the rest of the country may provide a basis for evaluating this association, given that Quebec has a lower level of economic vitality than does the rest of Canada (as reflected in various indicators, such as the rates of unemployment, poverty, welfare-dependency, etc.).

Muslims in Quebec

As has been mentioned, Quebec was one of the hotbeds of debates and tensions involving Muslims. The Bouchard-Taylor Report, which was published in 2007, concludes that the rising tension involving Muslims was mostly a media artifact, unaccompanied by any significant changes on the ground. Still, several studies indicate that the situation in Quebec is somewhat different from that in the rest of the country when it comes to the issue of immigrant communities. Indeed, using some of the measures discussed in this chapter, a comparison between Quebec and the rest of Canada indicates that Quebec is a special case when it comes to determining the status of its Muslim subpopulation.

Figure 7.13 shows the responses of Muslims in Quebec and in the rest of Canada with regard to several indicators of inter-group experiences. In Quebec, the rate at which Muslims reported having had bad experiences; having had concerns about unemployment, discrimination, and the future of Muslims in Canada; as well as having had the impression that Canadians have a generally negative impression of Islam are consistently higher than it is in the rest of Canada. The gap between Quebec and the rest of Canada hovers at around ten percentage points.

There are several potentially relevant factors that may help explain the differences between the experiences of Muslims in Quebec and those in the rest of Canada. One can think of language, culture and race, spatial segregation, secularism, the political environment, and economic conditions. Each of these factors could have some impact on the general social environment

FIGURE 7.13

Muslims' major concerns, comparing Quebec and the rest of Canada (ROC)

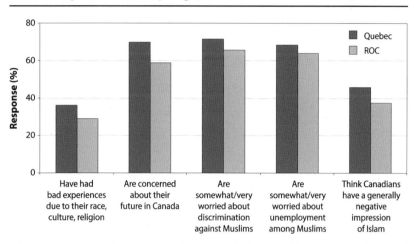

Source: Environics Institute, Survey of Canadian Muslims, 2006.

as well as on the ways in which immigrants are perceived to be influencing the local population.

Language is the most obvious factor here. English is the language of choice for the large majority of immigrants to Canada, including those who choose to settle in Quebec. While this is not a handicap in the rest of Canada, in Quebec it can lead to a greater degree of marginalization for all immigrants, including Muslims. It might also lower the level of communication and interaction between immigrants and the local population.

When language is not an issue – such as in the case of francophone immigrants – culture and race may be a more likely problem. The majority of Muslim French-speaking immigrants arrive from Lebanon and a couple of countries in North Africa. While sharing the language with the local population, these immigrants are very different from the host population in terms of cultural backgrounds and racial origins. As the example of the Herouxville Charter shows, differences in culture and lifestyle may be as potent as language in creating misunderstanding and tension between groups.

One particularly acute problem in Montreal, which is a favourite destination for immigrants to Quebec, is the high level of residential segregation along ethnic and cultural lines. For Muslims, such segregation means a reduced level of contact with the mainstream population and, as a consequence, lower exposure to the opportunities that that segment of the population offers. This can easily lead to a sense of alienation among Muslim immigrants.

Quebec is also the most secularized province in the country, a trend that started during Quebec's Quiet Revolution in the 1960s. Muslim immigrants, on the other hand, are among the most religious of immigrants (with some notable exceptions). This particular combination immediately draws a secular-religious fault line between Muslim immigrants and the local Quebecois population, who may worry about the erosion of the secular nature of their social environment and public institutions. Here again, the Herouxville Charter serves as a visible illustration of such a concern.

One unique feature of Quebec's political environment that may contribute to an uncomfortable relationship with immigrants is the presence of a separatist sentiment. During the various episodes of the sovereignty movement in Quebec there emerged a sentiment that made it clear that big segments of the separatist population see ethnic minorities as associated with the federalist camp; consequently, they are treated as an obstacle to Quebec separation. One manifestation of this may be found in the emotional comments made by Jacque Parizeau, Quebec's premier during the 1995 referendum on sovereignty. He blamed the defeat of the separatists on federal money and the "ethnic vote." Such sentiments would certainly affect the nature of the relationship between the local population and immigrants, including those of Muslim backgrounds.

Finally, the poorer economic conditions in the province could function to create stronger anti-minority and anti-immigrant sentiments. As has been the case in numerous periods of economic decline, in an environment of shrinking resources, the native-born segments of a population may treat immigrants as second-class citizens in an attempt to secure more economic opportunities for themselves. This may also partially explain the negative economic experiences of Muslims in Quebec.

As a result of the above factors, it is not surprising to see that, compared to the rest of Canada, in Quebec a smaller proportion of Muslim immigrants are prepared to adopt Canadian culture and customs. Regarding the question of whether immigrants should set aside their cultural backgrounds and adopt Canadian culture (Figure 7.14), the responses of Muslims in Quebec and Muslims in the rest of Canada are in opposition to one another. About 60 percent of respondents in Quebec disagree with this statement, which is about 25 percent higher than what is reported in the rest of Canada. There are also many more in Quebec than in the rest of Canada who feel ambivalent about agreeing to this statement. With regard to those

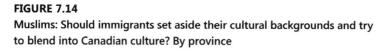

FIGURE 7.14
Muslims: Should immigrants set aside their cultural backgrounds and try
to blend into Canadian culture? By province

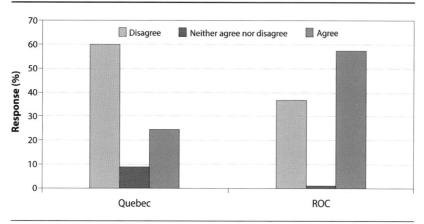

Source: Environics Institute, Survey of Canadian Muslims, 2006.

who agree, the difference between Quebec and the rest of Canada is more than 30 percent.

The comparisons between Quebec and the rest of Canada are also helpful for the purpose of predicting the future. Given the consistently higher levels of concerns among Muslims in Quebec regarding unemployment, discrimination, their future in Canada, negative impressions of Islam among Canadians, and the likelihood of having had bad experiences, and given the lower level of their willingness to integrate into Canadian culture, one could conclude that the exacerbation of those concerns in the rest of Canada would have similar consequences – that is, it would lower the level of Muslims' willingness to integrate into the Canadian culture in the country as a whole. In other words, the level of attachment to Canada reported by Quebec's Muslims can serve as an indicator of what the situation might look like in Canada as a whole if such concerns (employment, discrimination, etc.) grow among Muslims in the future.

The data presented in this chapter point to four major findings. First, unlike many other immigrant-receiving countries, in Canada the situation of Muslims is not critical and Muslims' levels of attachment to the country are fairly strong. The level of satisfaction with and engagement in societal affairs is quite high for Muslims, as it is for non-Muslims. Second, the inter-group comparisons show that, despite the generally high scores for all groups, Muslims are leaning towards the lower end of the scales on some crucial measures of attachment to Canada. The almost consistent nature of this pattern may signal the possibility of a more problematic attachment to Canada among Muslims. Third, the limited indicators available for suggesting future trends send an alarming signal that things might make a change for the worse if some outstanding issues remain unaddressed. Fourth, the situation of Muslims in Quebec is more problematic than it is in the rest of Canada.

What are the sources of the patterns discussed in this chapter and how could they possibly be addressed? To answer these questions we must take a closer look at the situation. This is the task of Part 4.

MUSLIMS IN CANADA: BACK STAGE

8

Muslims at Work

Digging Deeper into the Economy

In Chapter 7, we had a quick look at some of the measures of attachment to Canada among Muslims. The data show a relatively consistent deficit on the part of Muslims compared to people of other religious backgrounds and other immigrant groups. These measures range from the level of trust in the population to engagement in political processes, and from perceptions about the quality of life in Canada to life satisfaction and what the desire to come to Canada again would be given their current understanding. In more technical terms, these are "dependent variables." In this chapter and the next, I search for "independent variables," the factors behind the observed trends.

The data presented in Chapter 7 hint at a possible connection between the economic experiences of Muslims and their levels of attachment to Canada. Where Muslims face economic difficulties, there is a higher degree of concern about the rise of extremism, acknowledgment of the presence of discrimination, and worries about the future of Muslims in Canada. This clearly highlights the potential role played by economic factors. The centrality of economics in immigrants' lives in Canada is hardly surprising, given that a large majority of them are skilled workers whose primary goal in migrating was to prosper economically and whose main criterion for being granted admission to Canada was their economic potential. Against this backdrop, I now take a closer look at the economic experiences of Canadian Muslims and Muslim immigrants compared to those of native-born Canadians and other immigrants.

As we see throughout this chapter, the economic experiences of Canada's Muslim immigrants paint a picture that is distinct from those of many other immigrants. The core elements of this picture are twofold: (1) a generally lower-than-average performance by Muslims compared to immigrants of all other religious backgrounds and (2) the fact that this lower-than-average performance is not fully explained by human capital features (e.g., education, language skills, and prior job training and experience) or immigration-specific features (e.g., period of arrival and immigrant class).

Economic Experiences of Canadian Muslims

A thorough picture of a group's economic experiences may well require much more information than can be included in one chapter. I offer an outline of these experiences and attempt to show where the group stands with regard to the most general indicators of economic performance.

I start with the most fundamental indicators of economic performance: employment and income. Using the data from the Canadian Census of 2001, Figure 8.1 reports the average number of weeks worked in the previous year as well as the average income earned in that year. The 2001 census data are the latest available that include the variable "religion." As mentioned earlier, in the Canadian census, this variable is included in every other survey and the 2011 data are not yet available.

FIGURE 8.1
Average income and number of weeks worked in 2000, by religion

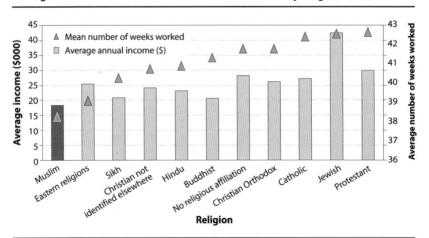

Source: Statistics Canada, Canadian Census, 2001.

FIGURE 8.2
Poverty rate (% below LICOs), by religion and immigration status, 2001

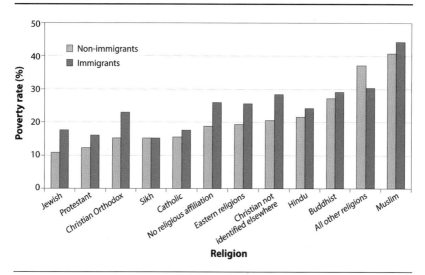

Source: Statistics Canada, Canadian Census, 2001.

The data in Figure 8.1 show that the two variables – weeks worked and average income – have a great degree of correlation. For both, Protestants, Jews, and Catholics are the top three groups, and Muslims are the bottom group. On average, Muslims worked about thirty-seven weeks throughout the year 2000, which is about six to seven weeks fewer than the group with the highest score. This equals an average of about two months of unemployment for every Muslim. The average income of Muslims is about $20,000, less than half of the incomes reported by the three groups with the highest annual incomes.

Figure 8.2 shows another important indicator of economic performance – the poverty rate. The numbers reported in this figure are the percentages of each group that lives below the poverty line as measured by Statistics Canada's low-income cut-offs (LICOs). Here, Muslims report the highest percentages. The inclusion of both immigrants and non-immigrants allows us to examine the extent to which the high rate of poverty among Muslims is related to their immigration status. The fact that the poverty rates for both immigrant and non-immigrant Muslims are the highest reported indicates that this is more than just a temporary, immigration-related issue. Another noteworthy feature in this figure is the fact that the poverty rates for Muslims are in the incredibly high levels of 40 to 45 percent.

FIGURE 8.3
Poverty rate (% below LICOs) of Muslims, by place of birth, 2001

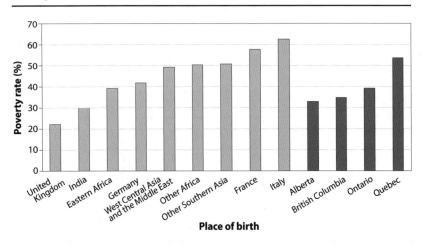

Source: Statistics Canada, Canadian Census, 2001.

The fact that the higher poverty rate of Muslims is not particularly related to immigration is further corroborated by comparing various subgroups within Muslims – for example, different generations and country of origin. Figure 8.3 reports the poverty rates of Muslims while separating them into those who were born outside Canada and those who were born inside the country; the former is then further broken down into the main countries or regions from which Muslim immigrants have come, and the latter is further broken down into various provinces with a sizeable Muslim population.

Figure 8.3 shows that the poverty rates of Muslim immigrants vary between a minimum of about 20 percent, for those who were born in the United Kingdom, to more than 60 percent, for those whose country of birth was Italy. All of the values in this range are significantly higher than the overall poverty rate of Canada – which was 12.5 percent in 2000 (Statistics Canada 2009, 87). But they are also higher than the poverty rate of all other immigrants, which, as reported in Figure 8.2, started at about 15 percent. The overwhelming majority of Muslims, however, come from three regions – Western Asia and the Middle East, India and Pakistan (the "Other Southern Asia" in Figure 8.3), and Eastern Africa – for whom the poverty rates are in the range of 40 to 50 percent. These are astonishingly high rates of poverty.

The poverty rates reported for second-generation Muslim immigrants – those born inside Canada, reported by the bars on the right hand side of Figure 8.3 – are no less surprising. The general expectation is that, due to their better command of the language and heightened familiarity and comfort with Canadian culture, as well as to their possessing Canadian educational credentials, the second-generation immigrants should have significantly lower rates of poverty than first-generation immigrants. Figure 8.3 partially confirms that expectation; however, the reported poverty rates for second-generation Muslims are still in the range of 30 to 55 percent, which is much higher than the national average. Among these, the two major areas of concentration for Canadian Muslims – Quebec and Ontario – have the highest poverty rates for second-generation Muslims.

The relatively high poverty rates of second-generation Muslim immigrants are of course curious, but they are also alarming. This is because things such as high rates of poverty and/or unemployment are exactly the kind of economic features that were found among second-generation Muslim immigrants in some European countries – countries that have some of the most alienated Muslim populations in the world. The November 2005 unrest in France, for instance, was most intense in deprived neighbourhoods in which younger Muslims had high unemployment and poverty rates. At first, the media and the law enforcement agencies tried to link these riots to identity challenges faced by young people of Arab-African descent who had become "French against their will"; however, later legislation (i.e., the Equal Opportunity Act) shows that at least part of the problem was related to economic disadvantages (Simon and Pala 2010, 100).

Another piece of alarming evidence surfaces when the poverty rates of Canadian Muslims are compared with those of Muslims living in other immigrant-receiving countries. The Pew Research Centre (2007, 3) has reported the differences in the low-income rates for Muslim minorities and the general populations of five industrial countries. In all those countries Muslims have a higher poverty rate, but there are significant variations between these countries: in the United States, Muslims have a poverty rate that is only 2 percent higher than that of the general public, while in France, Germany, Britain, and Spain, the difference is 18, 18, 22, and 23 percent, respectively. In Canada, the Muslim poverty rate is between 27 to 32 percent higher than the national poverty rate, which was around 12.5 percent in 2001. This is a gap that is higher than that of all other Western countries mentioned in the Pew report.

Patterned deprivation, especially if it cannot be explained by standard human capital factors or macroeconomic forces, provides fertile ground for the development of a sense of alienation. As Wuthnow (2002) shows in the case of the United States, the experience of economic marginalization quickly spills over into the social space and is reflected in the fact that all marginalized groups report lower levels of social capital. The sense of economic failure among these groups is often associated with a feeling that the broader society has failed to incorporate them into its ranks. This possibility is reinforced when such deprivation becomes more persistent and harder to escape.

An unusually high rate of poverty experienced by a group with distinct ethnic/racial features, particularly if the poverty appears inescapable, can quickly generate an ethnic/racial underclass. Often, such an underclass is defined not only by its high poverty rates but also by a distinct cultural outlook, which is the result of its poverty. In some cases, the consequences of this experience of poverty remain limited to the group itself – such as when it develops a so-called "culture of poverty," through which it normalizes its poverty and ceases to make efforts to break away from it. In other cases, poverty results in being disenfranchised from the broader society and in possibly taking extreme measures against the existing order (regarding how this applies to Canada and the United States, see Kazemipur and Halli 2000; Wilson 1987, 1997).

The timing of the data presented above does have certain implications. These data come from the 2001 Canadian census, which focuses on respondents' experiences in the preceding year. This places the census before the events of 11 September 2001, which were a turning point in the lives of Muslims in North America. These events unleashed a wave of Islamophobia in both the media and the larger population, and it would be very difficult to imagine that this wave had not had any impact on the economic lives of Muslims in Canada. Consequently, it is crucial to examine the changes that may have occurred since 2001.

Unfortunately, though, there are no systematic data comparable in size and quality to the Census 2001 data that might enable us to reliably detect possible changes in the post-9/11 decade. However, there is another Canadian dataset, smaller but with an exclusive focus on immigrants, that captures at least part of this period. This dataset – the LSIC – is based on information from about seventy-seven hundred immigrants who arrived in Canada in the year 2001. These immigrants were surveyed three times since their arrival: after six months (Wave 1), after two years (Wave 2), and after

FIGURE 8.4

Mean income, by religion and time

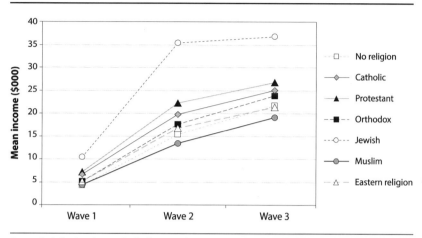

Source: Statistics Canada, Longitudinal Survey of Immigrants to Canada, 2005.

four years (Wave 3). The longitudinal nature of this data provides an extremely rare and rich glimpse into the experiences of immigrants in their new homes, particularly in the first few years after arrival, years that are crucial to setting the tone for their later lives in Canada.

The income profile of immigrants included in the LSIC survey strongly reinforces the picture given above. Figure 8.4 reports the average incomes of respondents belonging to seven different groupings: Protestants, Catholics, Orthodox, Jews, Muslims, Eastern religions, and no religion. The inclusion of the incomes for all three waves effectively reveals any possible changes in income over time. As the graph shows, in all three waves the lowest incomes are reported by Muslims; also, the gap in the average income of Muslims versus that in all other groups grows with the amount of time in Canada.

Some researchers may, for statistical reasons, be less comfortable with the use of mean income and may prefer median income as a more reliable income indicator. The rationale is that median scores are not heavily influenced by the presence of extremely high or low values and, therefore, report the centre of gravity for a variable without allowing for the possible influence of outliers. Due to the diversity of incomes reported by immigrants of different classes, this is a particularly likely possibility in the context of our discussion (e.g., refugees versus business-class immigrants). Repeating the above graph with boxplots – a statistical measure that reports not only the median values but also the variations around those values – reveals the exact same pattern. Not only that, the boxplots also show that the amount of variability of income among Muslim immigrants is much less than that for all other groups; that is, not only do Muslim immigrants have the lowest average incomes (i.e., a lower median value) but they are also more heavily concentrated around those lower incomes.

The significance of these data is that they report incomes while keeping several variables constant: all the respondents are immigrants (so there is no compounding of immigrant and the native-born); all have arrived in the same year (so there is no "period effect"); all had clearly declared their religious background (so there is no confusion between region of origin and religion). The patterns, therefore, seem even more reliable than those reported in the graphs based on census data.

Still, these patterns could have been influenced by another crucial variable not controlled for – that is, the immigrant class. Based on the type of visa granted to them, immigrants may be categorized under four main classes: (1) family class, referring to those who have been admitted to join family members already living in Canada; (2) refugees, referring to those who had to flee their countries of origin out of fear of persecution, war, or natural disaster; (3) business class, referring to a small group consisting of entrepreneurs and investors who come with relatively large financial resources; and, (4) skilled workers, referring to those admitted on the basis of their educational backgrounds and technical skills. Of these four groups, the first two tend to have more modest economic performances compared to the second two for the simple reason that the latter have been granted immigration visas on the basis of economic considerations. Also, skilled workers make up more than 50 percent of all immigrants. Due to these differences, it is important to examine the possible variations in the economic performances of immigrants while keeping the immigrant class constant. This is the basis of the data presented in Figure 8.5.

These figures report the mean income of Muslim immigrants versus that of immigrants of other religious backgrounds for each immigrant class and for each of the three waves. The graphs show that the general trend holds true here as well, generally so for refugee and family-class immigrants but particularly so for skilled workers. This is important because skilled workers are the largest segment of the immigrant population and are admitted with the understanding that they have enough human capital to function well in the job market. Business-class immigrants of Muslim background are the only anomaly here, in that they outperform all other immigrants admitted under business class.

FIGURE 8.5

Immigrant class: Mean income, by religion and time

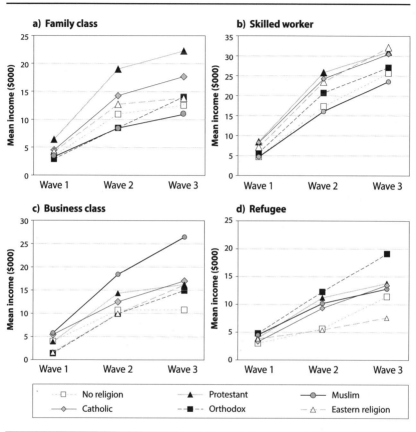

Source: Statistics Canada, Longitudinal Survey of Immigrants to Canada, 2005.

Here, two additional points are worth mentioning. First, in all three waves, refugee immigrants of Muslim background remain in the middle of the pack. This may speak to a better stock of human capital among them than among other groups. Second, the higher income reported by Muslim business-class immigrants does not necessarily signal better labour market integration; in many cases, this income is the result of self-employment or even dividends on investment holdings.

The income of business-class immigrants is dependent not only on the size of their capital but also on the extent of their entrepreneurial energy and creativity. They are mandated by immigration laws to establish a business shortly after arrival in Canada and to hire Canadian citizens. Thus, at worst they are self-employed and at best they are employers of other Canadians. In either case, they themselves do not need to be employed by someone else. They do not need to market themselves or their skills in order to be hired and to earn a living. For this reason, any possible labour market biases that might adversely affect other categories of immigrants do not affect business-class immigrants.

The flip side of this may be seen in the case of skilled-worker immigrants of Muslim backgrounds. In contrast to business-class Muslim immigrants, skilled-worker Muslim immigrants report the lowest incomes of all skilled-worker immigrants, whatever their religious backgrounds. And this is consistent throughout their first four years in Canada. This is also the case with family-class Muslim immigrants – immigrants who have to rely on their job market activities in order to earn a living.

The fact that the incomes reported by Muslim refugees are right in the middle of those reported by other refugees is also interesting. Refugees tend to go through a very different process than do other immigrants when they come to Canada. They mostly come through a third country, a country other than their native land, in which they have to wait until their refugee applications are processed. For many of them, this means the loss of their life savings. Also, for the most part, until their application is decided upon, they do not know to which country they will be sent. This is another disadvantage as they cannot prepare themselves ahead of time by learning about the culture and language of their destination country. The fact that, despite all these disadvantages, they perform reasonably well could point to the impact of the support they received in their first couple of years after arrival. Such support, either through government institutions, community organizations, or private sponsors, seems to help them stand on more solid ground than other groups of immigrants.

Another broad indicator of economic performance is employment status. The LSIC data allow for the examination of three employment-related indicators: the general employment rate, the full-time versus part-time nature of employment, and the duration of time before the acquisition of a job. Of these, the last is particularly important for immigrants as it marks the nature of their entrance into the labour market, which, in turn, sets their occupational trajectories for many years to come and also influences the outcomes of the other two indicators (with a longer waiting time, the chances of unemployment rises and the likelihood of taking any job, even part-time, increases).

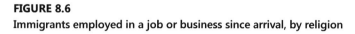

FIGURE 8.6
Immigrants employed in a job or business since arrival, by religion

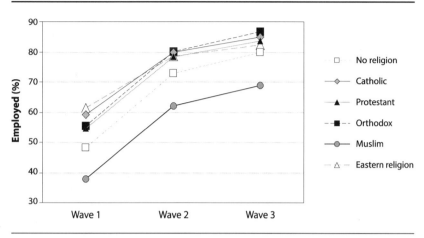

Source: Statistics Canada, Longitudinal Survey of Immigrants to Canada, 2005.

Perhaps the crudest employment measure is access to employment, regardless of whether it is part-time or full-time, whole-year or part-year, related to prior training or not. At this level, employment is simply a means towards making ends meet and providing for one's family. Figure 8.6 reports the status of immigrants of different faiths with regard to this particular employment indicator for all three waves. As the graph indicates, Muslim immigrants start with a rate of about 40 percent in the first wave, which rises to 70 percent in the third wave. While the rates show a rising trend for all groups, that for Muslims is consistently 10 to 20 percent lower than those for other groups.

Breaking down Figure 8.6 by immigrant class reveals a pattern more or less similar to the one we observed for income. Here again, Muslims report the lowest rates within each of the immigrant classes, with the exception of the business class, which reports a mid-range employment rate. However, the small size of the category of business-class immigrants, along with its unique employment needs, makes it difficult to draw any meaningful conclusion about it with regard to employment trends for the larger population.

A more informative measure of employment for immigrants is the amount of time between their arrival and the acquisition of their first job. The significance of this measure is twofold. First, the longer it takes for immigrants to find their first job, the more they have to rely on their savings;

FIGURE 8.7
Average number of months between arrival and first job, by religion

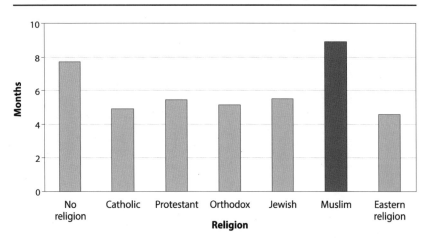

Source: Statistics Canada, Longitudinal Survey of Immigrants to Canada, 2005.

hence, with longer waiting periods, they are deprived of the capacity to absorb future possible economic shocks such as periods of unemployment due to recession, school attendance, or child-bearing. Second, having to wait a long time to acquire a job creates a strongly negative first impression of Canada, which is likely to last long after their employment difficulties have been overcome. Elsewhere, for instance, I show that a pleasant economic experience in an immigrant's initial years in Canada often translates into a long-lasting trust of Canadian society at large (see Kazemipur 2009). Clearly, initial employment experiences may be important both for their immediate economic effect and for their long-term socio-psychological effect.

Figure 8.7 shows the average number of months between arrival and the first job for the seven faith groups. The numbers vary between 4.5 months for Eastern religions to slightly less than nine months for Muslim immigrants. Given the fact that the majority of those immigrants are skilled workers who depend on their employment for income, and that the graph reports the numbers for the third wave (i.e., after four years in Canada), this means that the average Muslim immigrant waits nine months before getting his/her first job. Looked at differently, he/she looks for employment for approximately 20 percent of his/her first four years – a waiting period that comes immediately after the stress of migration.

Examining the same indicator of economic performance separately for each immigrant class shows that, with the exception of refugee-class immigrants, the long periods of unemployment after arrival remain consistent for skilled-worker Muslim immigrants (almost tied with no religion) but are particularly high for family-class immigrants, who make up a larger proportion of Muslim immigrants than do other groups. So on this economic performance indicator, too, Muslims score consistently low.

The data examined thus far seem to present a clear image – one in which Muslims score lower than other immigrant groups, with the differences being significant and consistent. The data also show that such differences cannot be easily explained by the presence of a higher number of refugee- or family-class immigrants among Muslims because the patterns remain more or less the same within each category. Nor is the period effect a factor as all these immigrants arrived in the same year. In our search for the forces behind these patterns, we first explore the most obvious: human capital.

Human Capital in the Making of Economic Capital?

Human capital – manifested through formal education, language skills, occupational training, and so on – is closely related to economic capital. While many factors could be at work to create a particular economic outcome, in modern economies human capital is among the most immediate and influential. The growth of the service industry and the shift to what is nowadays called the "knowledge economy" have created enormous demands for human capital, entailing a drastic shift from a time when physical labour was the main commodity in demand.

The connection between economic and human capital can clearly be seen in the responses of immigrants to a question regarding the most significant difficulty they have faced in Canada. The two most frequently cited answers are related to economic and human capital. Figure 8.8 reports that about 40 percent of all immigrants consider their most serious difficulty to be that of finding a job, immediately followed by learning the official languages (about 20 percent). There is good reason to think of economic and human capital as related to one another when it comes to the lives of immigrants. Many studies have shown the significant impact of language barriers on immigrants' occupational trajectories. In other words, when faced with a language barrier, immigrants aim for the type of employment that does not require strong communication skills, and most such jobs tend to be found either in low-paying sectors of the economy or in ethnic enclaves.

FIGURE 8.8

Most important difficulty since arrival in Canada, all immigrants

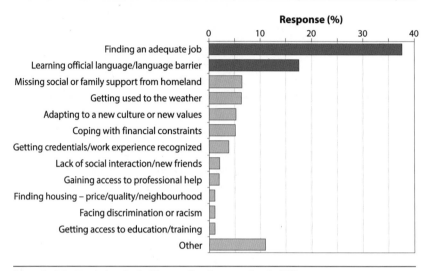

Source: Statistics Canada, Longitudinal Survey of Immigrants to Canada, 2005.

Given the general connection between economic performance and language skills, one may wonder about the extent to which the lower economic performance of Muslim immigrants could be attributed to a high degree of difficulty with regard to learning the country's official languages. However, Figures 8.12 and 8.13 imply that this may not necessarily be the case for Muslim immigrants. While Figure 8.9 confirms that, compared to all other groups, Muslim immigrants face the most acute level of employment-related challenge (a finding that was also conveyed through the data presented earlier in this chapter), Figure 8.10 shows that Muslims report the lowest level of language difficulties. This implies that the economic challenges faced by Muslims do not directly stem from their human capital, at least insofar as language skills are concerned. So, while poor economic performances can often be related to poor language skills, this does not seem to be the case with Muslim immigrants: language skills cannot adequately explain the economic trends seen earlier.

But human capital is much more than just language skills. The hypothesis that the poor economic performance of Muslim immigrants may be due to their lower stock of human capital needs to be verified by examining the impact of formal education. Figure 8.11 shows the distribution of the six

FIGURE 8.9

Most important difficulty since arrival, by religion: Finding an adequate job

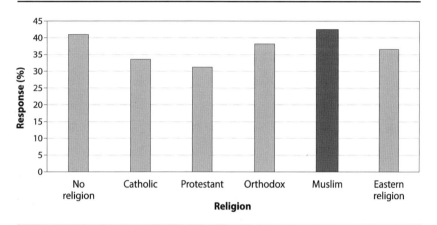

Source: Statistics Canada, Longitudinal Survey of Immigrants to Canada, 2005.

FIGURE 8.10

Most important difficulty since arrival, by religion: Language barrier

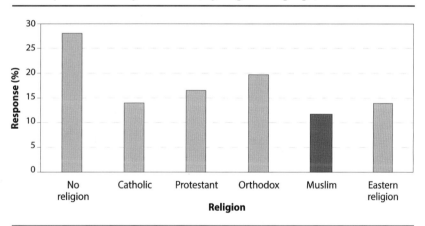

Source: Statistics Canada, Longitudinal Survey of Immigrants to Canada, 2005.

more populous faith groups according to different ranks of formal education, reported under five broad categories. A quick look at the educational profiles of different groups reveals something that could have an impact on their earnings – the presence of a higher proportion of people with a high school diploma or less among Muslim and Eastern religion immigrants.

FIGURE 8.11

Highest level of education, by religion

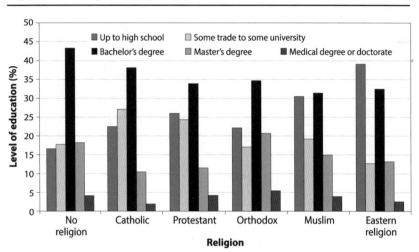

Source: Statistics Canada, Longitudinal Survey of Immigrants to Canada, 2005.

Could this explain the income and employment trends discussed earlier? Not quite. To explain this, we need to consider two additional points.

The first point to consider involves the source of this particular anomaly with regard to Muslim and Eastern religions immigrants. As mentioned earlier, immigrants are admitted under different categories, and these categories have different human capital profiles: refugee and family-class immigrants tend to come with the lowest average education, and skilled workers with the highest. For this reason, a large number of refugee and family-class immigrants within a faith group pushes the average education score down for that group. This is precisely the case for Muslim and Eastern religions immigrants. Given this, is it plausible to attribute the poorer economic performance of Muslim immigrants as a group to their higher proportion of less-educated refugee and family-class immigrants? The answer is still no, and this is because Muslim immigrants report a lower income even when the immigrant class is kept constant (at least with regard to the skilled-worker class and the family class). In other words, Muslim immigrants have lower income and poorer employment trajectories even when the better-educated skilled workers and less-educated family-class immigrants are compared with their counterparts in other groups. The differences remain even when education is taken into account.

The second point with regard to the potential impact of education on the economic performance of immigrants is related to the differences between Muslim immigrants and Eastern religions immigrants. A close comparison of the educational profiles of these two groups shows that their proportional distribution in higher education categories are fairly similar; however, in less-than-university categories, Eastern religions immigrants have a much higher proportion of those with educational attainments that are only up to high school. Despite this comparative advantage, Muslim immigrants perform much lower than Eastern religions immigrants in the areas of income and employment. If education is the explanatory factor here, we should see the opposite.

In sum, combining the income and educational profiles of various groups of immigrants does not seem to support the argument that lower levels of income among Muslim immigrants are due to lower education. Nor is it plausible to attribute this to a higher proportion of those with foreign credentials (as this is an attribute of all immigrants), or a higher proportion of family- and refugee-class immigrants (as the differences remain after controlling for immigrant class), or the timing of their arrival (as the LSIC survey participants all arrived at the same time). Thus, the quest for a plausible explanation must continue.

A distinction could be made here between one's level of education and one's ability to turn that education into employment and income. It is quite possible to imagine that two individuals or groups with similar levels of education perform quite differently economically due to their different ability to translate their human capital into economic gains. In other words, the differences would be not in the amount of education they have but, rather, in the levels of return on their education (i.e., the monetary rewards due to their educational qualifications). To what extent could this explain the economic disadvantage experienced by Muslim immigrants?

Figure 8.12 allows for an indirect examination of this question by showing the differences between the income and education of immigrants of different religious backgrounds. Education is measured through the highest credentials attained, organized on the x-axis from the lowest to the highest, with the y-axis reporting the average income for those in each education category. Each of the three figures shows this relationship for one of the three waves of immigration to Canada (after six months, two years, and four years in the country, respectively). Comparing the trend lines shown in these three figures could indicate possible changes in the dynamics of the relationship between education and income during the crucial first few years in Canada.

FIGURE 8.12

Mean income trendlines at Wave 1, Wave2, and Wave 3, by highest level
of education and religion

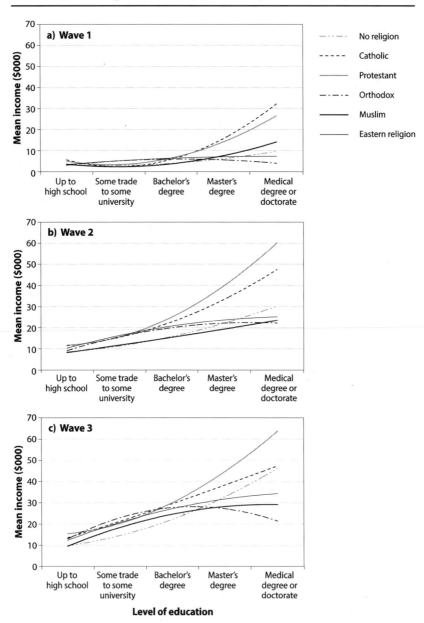

As expected, for all the groups included, the range of incomes reported in the first wave is naturally lower than that in the other two waves. This range of values goes up with each wave, reflecting the general improvement in the incomes of immigrants the longer they stay in Canada. Another expected feature of these graphs is that the trend lines follow an exponential pattern, indicating that the rate of return is even greater in the higher educational levels. In other words, attaining one additional year of postsecondary education, for instance, adds much more to one's income than attaining one additional year of high school education. This is a pattern that remains consistent for almost all groups and throughout the three waves.

A comparison of the trend lines for Muslims for the three waves, however, reveals an anomaly. While the trend line for Muslims after their first six months in Canada follows an exponentially rising pattern – the same as most of the other groups – in the second wave the exponential nature of the trend line turns into a straight line. The line is still rising, indicating that those with more education will earn more, but in a linear fashion, as opposed to the exponential fashion present in the previous wave. So, while for most others, one year of university education yields a much higher return than does one year of non-university education, this difference disappears for Muslim immigrants. More important, by the third wave (i.e., four years after immigrating) the trend line plateaus and starts to decline. This means that, from a certain point on, for Muslims any additional university education will not yield extra economic gains and might even erode some of their earnings (if the trend continues in the same fashion). This unique pattern for Muslims occurs while the rising exponential trends continue for all other groups, with the exception of Orthodox immigrants.

What this indicates is that, for Muslim immigrants, the return to education is not the same as it is for other immigrant groups. This, combined with the fact that a much smaller proportion of Muslim immigrants reported struggling with language barriers, would imply that a lower return on human capital could be one of the sources of the unusually high degree of economic difficulties faced by Muslims. But there is more to human capital than formal education.

It has been argued that informal education and on-the-job training sometimes pays off more than formal school-based education. Those who have more work experience but less formal education, according to this line of argument, may do better in the job market than those with the opposite portfolio. This is particularly relevant in the case of immigrants to Canada because they have to secure a minimum number of employment points prior

FIGURE 8.13

Proportion of immigrants who worked before coming to Canada, by gender and religion

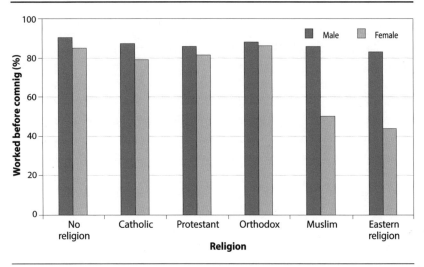

Source: Statistics Canada, Longitudinal Survey of Immigrants to Canada, 2005.

to applying for immigration (without these points their application would be automatically rejected). It is therefore reasonable to ask whether the poorer job market performance of Muslim immigrants is a consequence of their lack of work experience before migration. But again, this is not the case.

Figure 8.13 reports the proportion of immigrants who had worked before coming to Canada. It separates men and women of various religious categories in order to disallow the possible compounding effects due to differential rates of male/female employment. This figure shows a couple of interesting and important things. First, the percentages are lower for women of all religious backgrounds. Second, gender differences are particularly noticeable for those of Muslim and Eastern religions backgrounds, hovering around thirty-some percentage points. Third, for immigrant women of the last two groups, there is about a ten percentage point difference between their pre-migration employment rates, with women of Eastern religions backgrounds reporting the lowest level. Last, the rates reported for men are very close to each other, all fluctuating in the 80 percent range. If these differences are responsible for post-migration economic experiences, we should see a corresponding difference in the post-migration rates for all the groups.

FIGURE 8.14

Proportion of males who have been employed since arrival, by religion

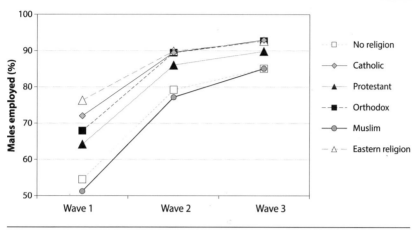

Source: Statistics Canada, Longitudinal Survey of Immigrants to Canada, 2005.

FIGURE 8.15

Proportion of females who have been employed since arrival, by religion

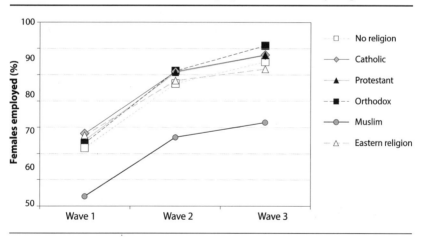

Source: Statistics Canada, Longitudinal Survey of Immigrants to Canada, 2005.

To examine the degree of correspondence between pre- and post-migration economic experiences, we included in Figures 8.14 and 8.15 the percentage of immigrants who have been employed – any kind of employment – since their arrival. These rates are reported for men and women separately in order to defray any possible confounding effect. The post-migration trends for employment rates show the consistent differences between men and women, with about a ten percentage point difference in the lowest and highest rates reported for men and women, reflecting a similar difference in their pre-migration experiences. In terms of religion, two things are noteworthy: (1) both Muslim men and Muslim women report the lowest rates and (2) Muslim women report the lowest level of all, with a wide margin of about twenty percentage points between them and all other immigrant women. If the pre-migration poor employment records are supposed to duplicate themselves after migration, it should be women of Eastern religions background – not Muslim women – who report the lowest employment rates after migration. But this is not the case. The fact that Muslim women are reporting the lowest post-migration employment rates, and by a wide margin, weakens the argument regarding the correspondence between pre- and post-migration employment experiences as an explanation for Muslim immigrants' lower income and employment in Canada.

When we examine the waiting time until the first job, a more or less similar pattern surfaces. Here again, the rates are consistently higher for women than for men, with Muslims having to wait the longest in both categories and with Muslim immigrant women having to wait longest of all. The immigrant group next to Muslim women is Jewish women. However, this proximity may not be an indicator of similarity of experiences as, by a wide margin, Jewish immigrant men report the shortest waiting time and the highest average income. The longer waiting period for Jewish immigrant women, therefore, might be a reflection of a conscious decision on their part to start their employment at a later time. In either case, the small number of Jewish immigrants prohibits any further exploration of the reasons for their waiting time.

There is yet another angle to the issue of the correspondence between pre- and post-migration experiences, and that is related to the degree to which those who have worked before migration could transfer their work experiences to the new job market. As Figure 8.16 shows, Muslims report the highest percentage of immigrants whose out-of-Canada work experiences have not counted in their host country. What is visible here is the increasing gap between Muslims and all other immigrants the longer they stay in Canada, reaching a difference of about 20 percent by the end of their fourth year in Canada.

When looked at as a whole, the above information points to the possibility that the atypical economic experiences of Muslim immigrants cannot be reduced to lower education, non-recognition of foreign credentials, lack of

FIGURE 8.16

Outside work experience has not been accepted, by religion and time

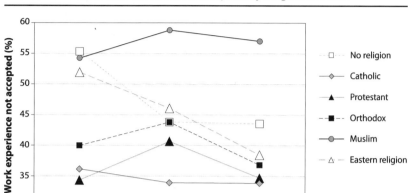

Source: Statistics Canada, Longitudinal Survey of Immigrants to Canada, 2005.

pre-migration work experience, immigrant class, period of arrival, age at arrival, and so on. Nor do they have much to do with technical aspects of their education, such as the field of study, as all immigrants go through the same point system before they are admitted to Canada. Nor are they due to a lower level of language skills among Muslim immigrants. What does seem to be relevant with regard to explaining these atypical economic experiences is a lower level of return on education and the non-recognition of pre-migration work experiences. These factors, however, are more than just technical and market-related forces: they are mostly social in nature.

From Economy to Social Economy

Scholars in the field of social economy have long shown that economic machinery does not run merely on technical wheels; rather, a variety of social elements need to be in place before an economy can function smoothly. Putnam (1994, 2001), for instance, shows the centrality of social trust to economic prosperity and to the efficient working of economic machinery. Burt (1995) also studies the significant role that social networks play in the economic domain. Besides these macro-level aspects, the importance of the "social" in the functioning of the economy is evident even at the micro level: everyone who has ever attended or conducted a job interview knows that the social desirability of the interviewees and the personal likes and dislikes of the interviewers can be as influential as the applicant's technical competencies and professional skills. In other words, not everything that is happening in the job market can necessarily be explained by reference to economic variables.

Against this background, it is reasonable to expect, at least theoretically, that the culprits behind the particular experiences of Muslim immigrants in the Canadian economy might have to be sought in the social/communal domain – that is, in the nature of the personal relationships and social ties developed between Muslims and the mainstream population. Such relationships do not have to initially occur in the workplace: they can easily be formed in neighbourhoods and schools. Once shaped, they have the potential to spill over into the labour market. Personal likes and dislikes play a role in the job market.

Clear evidence for the presence of the social in the economy is presented in a study conducted by Oreopoulos (2009). In this study, six thousand resumes were sent to potential employers in Canada, with various styles of naming, including hyphenated names. Controlling for all the technical aspects, the study found that the applicants with English-sounding first and last names received the most interview invitations by a considerable margin. These were followed by those with mixed English-foreign names, and last were those with foreign-sounding first and last names. The author's conclusion is that, "overall, the results suggest considerable employer discrimination against applicants with ethnic names or with experience from foreign firms" (5).

One piece of evidence in our data speaks to the presence of the social in the economy in a very general way. Looking at the intersection of Muslim concerns about the occurrence of Muslim unemployment and the good or bad nature of the experiences related to their religion, race, or ethnicity (Figure 8.17) shows that the two are generally correlated: those who have had bad experiences are much more likely to be worried about unemployment than are those who have had good experiences. There is a valid reason for this connection as the potentially good or bad experiences related to culture do not occur in a vacuum; rather, they occur as a result of interactions with others in a variety of settings (e.g., the neighbourhood, the school, the workplace).

In sum, each economy functions within, and has a give-and-take relationship with, a social environment; hence, economic activities may easily be influenced by the social environments within which they operate. It is important to explore this for policy-making reasons since there is little

FIGURE 8.17

Muslims: Correlation of the nature of experiences about their race, ethnicity, or religion and how worried they are about Muslim unemployment

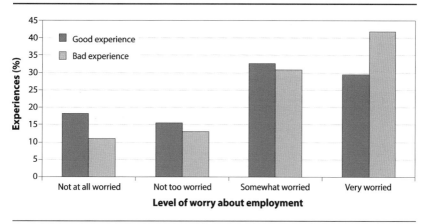

Source: Environics Institute, Survey of Canadian Muslims, 2006.

point in fixing a technical economic issue if the source of the problem lies in the social domain. It is against this backdrop that, in the next chapter, I examine the communal aspect of the integration of Muslim immigrants into Canada.

I should, however, preface this with the caveat that most of the dynamics in the social domain are subtle and therefore difficult to capture. The limitations of the existing data add to this difficulty. Keeping this in mind, I hope to capture at least some of these dynamics.

9

Beyond the Friendly Smiles

Muslims in the Community

To be able to function normally, one has to maintain a minimum level of engagement with one's surrounding community. The absence of such engagement would immediately reveal its impact not only in one's psychological state but also in all other areas of life, whether economic, political, or cultural. Recent scholarship on social capital convincingly illustrates this. Quite often, however, people do not fully understand the extent of their own social engagement, nor do they appreciate its impact on their lives. This is particularly so in Western countries, due partly to the prevalence of individualism but also to the fact that social connections shape themselves gradually and inconspicuously, often not having a clear starting or ending point. For this reason, they may remain in the background for a long time (for a thorough discussion of social capital, see Putnam 2001).

For immigrants, however, the situation is different simply because migration abruptly resets their social and communal world. Sometimes in a span of only twenty-four hours – the maximum time needed for a trip from the Old Country to the New Country – they experience a complete loss of common cultural codes for social conduct, the language needed for communication, the physical and emotional support of social networks, and people with whom they had a shared history and who had provided them with a sense of comfort and identity. Immigrants, therefore, are fully aware of the beginning and the ending of their social connections – and the great challenges that come with this.

Starting a new relationship is always difficult, and building a whole set of social relationships is even more difficult. For immigrants, this process is intensified because they have to develop social connections while crossing language barriers, cultural differences, and various social statuses. No matter how advanced an immigrant's language skills, they cannot equip her/him with the level of comfort needed to enter a social relationship with people in the mainstream population. No matter how culturally informed an immigrant may be, he or she still needs a great deal of time to fully absorb all the cultural codes and symbols in the new society. No matter how successful and established an immigrant might have been in his or her home country, he/she always enters the new society as someone with no status. The social infrastructure needed for the development of long-term social ties is simply not there for immigrants upon arrival.

And this is only one side of the equation. If social ties are to develop, there is a need for another willing party. This party, in the case of immigrants, is the mainstream population. It is often said that the integration of immigrants is a two-way process: nowhere is this more clear than in the development of social relationships. The biggest challenge here is the fact that the two parties enter the scene from very different positions. On the one hand, there are immigrants, who have lost all their social networks and are badly in need of developing new ones; on the other, there is the host population, who, for the most part, feel no need to develop any social ties with immigrants. What is more, in certain environments, members of the mainstream population may dislike the fact that immigrants are there, viewing them as competitors for their jobs or even as threats to their lifestyles.

Sometimes immigrants have to initiate interaction with a host population that has no desire to engage with them. This occurs in the case of those groups of immigrants about whom the host population already holds negative images, stereotypes, and narratives. In such cases, immigrants are at a great disadvantage and social connections shape up very slowly, if ever.

To enter into social relationships with the host population, Muslim immigrants to Canada have not only to overcome the barriers faced by all other immigrants but also to fight an uphill battle against an environment that is clearly biased against Muslims. In order to develop a simple relationship, they have to break through the images and narratives that are daily dispatched and reinforced by the media. In circumstances like this, a relationship with the native-born population does not start from zero: it starts from a deficit.

FIGURE 9.1

Proportion who have volunteered time to a religious activity, by religion and time

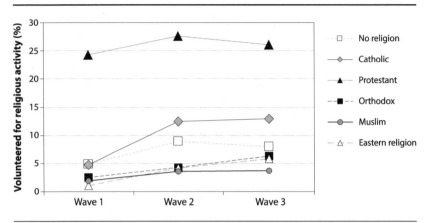

Source: Statistics Canada, Longitudinal Survey of Immigrants to Canada, 2005.

The popular media often portray Muslims as a group that prefers to concentrate in its own religious circles, secluded from both the mainstream population and other immigrants. The assumption is that, for Muslims, religion plays a crucial role in shaping their thoughts, opinions, and daily behaviours. It follows that, normally, Muslims show a much higher level of engagement with members of their faith community than with members of the broader community. Figure 9.1, however, shows a very different picture. Asking immigrants whether or not they have volunteered any time to a religious activity of any sort allows us to compare the centrality of religion for different groups of immigrants. As the figure shows, Muslims report the lowest percentages of all faith groups (less than 5 percent), while the highest percentage is reported by Protestants, followed by Catholics and Eastern religions immigrants. For Muslims, the reported percentages remain fairly stable throughout the three waves of the LSIC data.

The above trends should be understood against the backdrop of the rising significance of religion for immigrants in the post-migration phase. Experiencing the loss of their communities and social networks, immigrants tend to turn to religious communities in their new homes as a readily available substitute, something that will enable them to satisfy their emotional need for belonging and connection as well as for material support during the settlement process. This is probably the reason that, sometimes, even immigrants with no particular religious affiliation start participating in

FIGURE 9.2

Frequency of Muslims' religious participation, by time

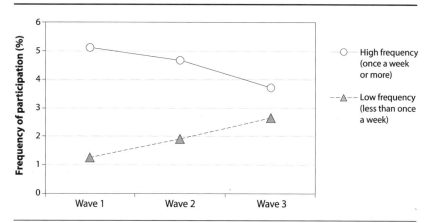

Source: Statistics Canada, Longitudinal Survey of Immigrants to Canada, 2005.

religion-based activities after migration. Interestingly enough, however, as Figure 9.1 shows, by the third wave the rate for Muslims falls below even that of the no religion immigrants.

A similar trend is found with regard to Muslim immigrants' participation in religious functions. Figure 9.2 shows the percentage of Muslims with high and low frequencies of such participation. Not only are the percentages reported for the high frequency rate (once a week or more) quite low (5 percent or less), they decline even further in the first four years after arrival. The percentages of those who attend such functions rises only infrequently.

Religion, however, is only one component of one's cultural heritage; ethnicity is another. If Muslims are not spending a great deal of time on purely religious functions and activities, are they spending more time with their co-ethnics? This is a relevant question because such a tendency has been shown to be prevalent among immigrants of various ethnic/cultural backgrounds. This tendency is measured in several different ways, but mostly it is measured according to the degree to which people reside in neighbourhoods containing a large population of their co-ethnics. Figure 9.3 shows that Muslims rank second lowest in terms of the proportion of the group's population who share a neighbourhood with co-ethnics. The reported percentage for Muslims is about one-third of that for Eastern religions and no religion backgrounds. A similar pattern surfaces with regard to the question on sharing a neighbourhood with immigrants in general (not shown here).

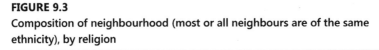

FIGURE 9.3

Composition of neighbourhood (most or all neighbours are of the same ethnicity), by religion

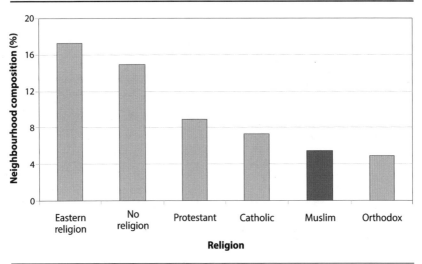

Source: Statistics Canada, Longitudinal Survey of Immigrants to Canada, 2005.

The low frequency of participation in religious functions for Muslims, combined with the low percentage of their population who live in neighbourhoods with large concentrations of co-ethnics, indicates that Muslims do not necessarily have a tendency to stay away from mainstream society and to stay within their own religious, ethnic, or immigrant circles. By virtue of living in a wide range of neighbourhoods, Muslims are reasonably exposed to members of the mainstream population and are open for engagement and interaction with them. To what extent could this openness be said to have actually resulted in the development of social relationships with the mainstream population?

Figure 9.4 shows the level of contact that native-born Canadians have reported with members of different ethnic/religious groups. The data show three distinct patterns: (1) a relatively high level of contact with those of anglophone/francophone, Black, Chinese, and Aboriginal backgrounds; (2) a balanced distribution of low/high contact with those of Jewish, Pakistani, and East Indian backgrounds; and (3) a low level of contact with Muslims. About 35 percent of native-born Canadians seem to have had no contact with any Muslim – a significantly high percentage when compared to all other groups.

FIGURE 9.4

Canadians' level of contact with different minority groups

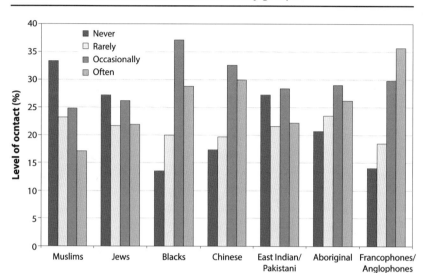

Source: Environics Institute, Survey of Canadian Muslims, 2003.

This low level of contact between native-born Canadians and Muslims has consequences for the integration of Muslims into Canadian communal life. As discussed in previous chapters, social contact between members of different groups leads to the weakening of inter-group stereotypes and the development of mutually positive attitudes. Conversely, the lack of such contact tends to prolong the lives of negative stereotypes, which then hinders the formation of any future long-term relationships.

One oft-cited function of stereotypes is that they facilitate the spread of discrimination against minorities. Do Canadian Muslims suffer from discrimination? Theoretically, a group may be subjected to discriminatory treatment on the basis of one or more of their features (e.g., religious background, cultural/ethnic origin, race and skin colour, sexual orientation, language, and gender). The existing data allow us to examine the extent of this phenomenon with regard to Muslim immigrants in the areas of religion, ethnicity/culture, and race.

Figure 9.5 reports, for all immigrants and for skilled workers, the percentage of survey respondents who felt that they had been subjected to discriminatory treatment on the basis of their religion. One piece of good news about the reported trends is that the rates are generally low, less than

FIGURE 9.5

Proportion of immigrants who faced religious discrimination, by religion
and time

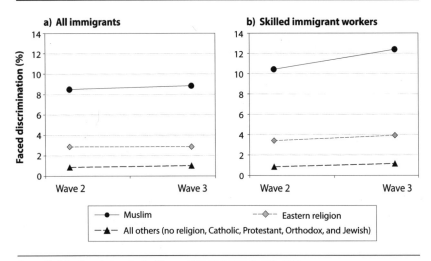

Source: Statistics Canada, Longitudinal Survey of Immigrants to Canada, 2005.

13 percent (which forces us, due to Statistics Canada's regulations, to combine several groups with small cell counts in order to be able to include
them in the graphs). Within that relatively low range, however, there is a big
gap between the rates reported by Muslims and those reported by all other
groups. As the graph illustrates, while the trends are relatively stable for
other groups of immigrants, they seem to be rising for Muslims; and this
rise is even more pronounced for skilled workers.

An indicator closely related to discrimination on the basis of religion is
discrimination on the basis of ethnic/cultural background. As Figure 9.6
shows, unlike the former, in this regard Muslim immigrants are not visibly
distinct from other immigrants. Actually, in Wave 2 (two years after landing
in Canada) it is Protestant immigrants who report receiving the highest
percentage of this kind of treatment. However, two years later, the rate for
Protestant immigrants drops noticeably (from about 17 to 12 percent) while
that of Muslim immigrants takes its place. Thus, by Wave 3 of the survey
(four years after landing in Canada), Muslim immigrants are the group
with the highest percentage reporting having been subject to discrimination
on the basis of ethnic/cultural background. Like the previous indicator,
this trend is even more pronounced for Muslim immigrants in the skilled-
worker category (not shown here).

FIGURE 9.6
Proportion of immigrants who faced ethnic/cultural discrimination, by religion and time

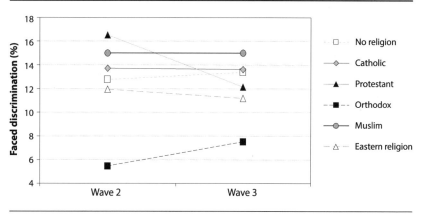

Source: Statistics Canada, Longitudinal Survey of Immigrants to Canada, 2005.

The next indicator of self-perceived discrimination is that which is based on race and skin colour, and it is reported in Figure 9.7. The figure reveals a distinct and interesting pattern in that Muslim immigrants report the lowest rates at the end of their second year and at the end of their fourth year in Canada; but, unlike all other groups, for whom the trend line is declining, for Muslims it is rising. Unfortunately, the data do not go beyond the fourth

FIGURE 9.7
Proportion of immigrants who faced racial discrimination, by religion and time

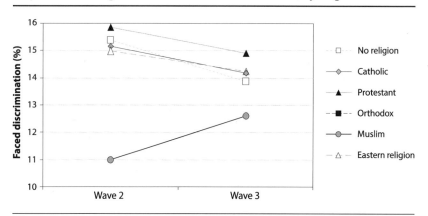

Source: Statistics Canada, Longitudinal Survey of Immigrants to Canada, 2005.

year; however, if these trends continue in the same fashion, then, by their sixth year in Canada, the rate reported by Muslims will be the highest.

The data presented above show that Muslim immigrants consistently experience either an already high level of discrimination or a level that is low but noticeably rising. The use of multiple indicators of discrimination gives us some assurance about the reliability of the data presented so far. However, given the importance of the issue of discrimination and the complexity of the task of measuring it, we should not be content with using only one data set. Also, we should not rely merely on indicators of self-perceived discrimination, as those self-perceptions may not accurately reflect the reality. It is therefore necessary to further analyze this important issue.

Let us first look at what other data can tell us. In a survey conducted by Environics, shown in Figure 9.8, about 65 percent of Muslims report being either somewhat worried or very worried about discrimination against Muslims living in Canada. Comparing this number with those based on the LSIC data raises an interesting point. The Environics numbers are significantly higher than those reported by recent immigrants in the LSIC data. While in the LSIC data the percentage of recent Muslim immigrants worrying about various types of discrimination never reaches the 20 percent mark, the Environics data indicate 35 and 30 percent, respectively, for each of the top two categories. It is important to note that the Environics data are based on a sample of all Muslim Canadians, while LSIC refers only to recent immigrants. It is also important to note that the trends reported in the LSIC data are all rising for Muslims. This may be taken to suggest that, with longer stays in Canada, Muslims become more subject to – or more aware of – discrimination. The confirmation of similar results through the data from a different survey adds to our confidence that what we are observing is a real trend and not just a statistical artifact.

Still, there are problems. There is always a possibility that those who report being victims of a certain type of discrimination are doing so in an attempt to excuse their own failures or lack of achievement. In these cases, people tend to over-report and to exaggerate actual and experienced levels of discrimination. To reach a conclusion about the prevalence of discrimination against a particular group based solely on its members' self-perceived reports is dubious at best. As important as it is to capture the sentiment and opinions of people on the receiving end of discriminatory acts, it is more important (and interesting) to see things from the perspective of those on the giving end of such practices – that is, from the perspective of the majority population.

FIGURE 9.8

Muslims: How worried are you about discrimination against Muslims living in Canada?

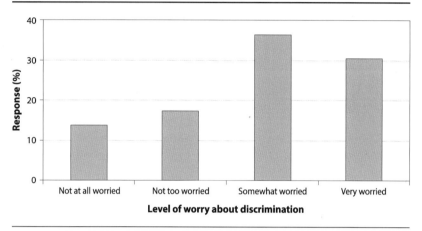

Level of worry about discrimination

Source: Environics Institute, Survey of Canadian Muslims, 2006.

FIGURE 9.9

Canadians: How often do you think Muslims are subject to discrimination in Canadian society today?

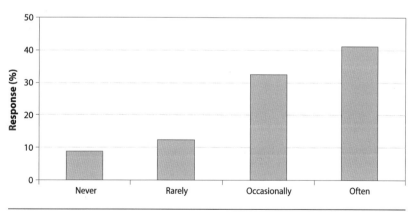

Source: Environics Institute, Survey of Canadian Muslims, 2006.

Figure 9.9 reports the distribution of answers of native-born Canadians to the question of how often they think Muslims are subjected to discrimination in Canada. Interestingly enough, about 75 percent of Canadians think that Muslims are either occasionally or often subjected to discrimination in today's society. Comparing this number with those reported by Muslims

themselves, and assuming that the top two categories refer to the same phenomenon (despite the different wording), one can see that, by a margin of
about ten percentage points, more native-born Canadians than Muslims
acknowledge the existence of discrimination against Muslims. The fact that
Canadians' views on the frequency of discrimination against Muslims are
so close to the views expressed by Muslims themselves serves as a partial
and indirect confirmation of the magnitude and seriousness of the issue,
signifying that what Muslims feel is not merely an excuse for their possible
failure in other areas.

One might still wonder, however, about the extent to which the views of
native-born Canadians might reflect their care and empathy for Muslims
and/or their interest in Islam rather than their objective observations. Given
this, it is worth breaking down the answers of native-born Canadians according to the degree of their interest in Islam in order to detect the possible
influence of these interests on their opinions.

Figure 9.10 divides the answers of native-born Canadians regarding the
frequency of discrimination against Muslims according to their impressions
of Islam, which are categorized as positive, negative, or neither. Interestingly
enough, the numbers remain virtually unchanged for the different categories

FIGURE 9.10

Canadians: How often do you think Muslims are the subject of discrimination
in Canadian society today? By general impression of Islam

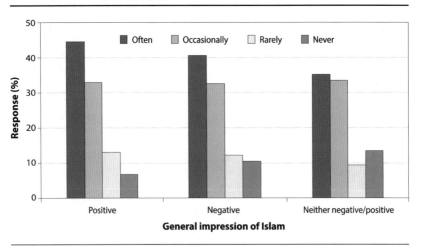

Source: Environics Institute, Survey of Canadian Muslims, 2006.

of "impression of Islam," with the total percentage of "often" and "occasionally" hovering around 70 to 80 percent. In other words, whether native-born Canadians like or dislike Islam does not change their views regarding the high level of discrimination that Muslims face in Canadian society.

The last two findings – (1) that native-born Canadians acknowledge the prevalence of discrimination against Muslims almost as frequently as do Muslims themselves and (2) that such acknowledgement is not affected by their views on Islam – are important. They suggest that what is being reported by Muslims is not just a subjective perception with no basis in reality but, rather, that it alludes to the existence of a real and serious phenomenon. It reveals an important element in the nature of the relationship between Muslim immigrants and the native-born population in Canada – an element that needs to be taken into account when we think about how this relationship might be improved. The findings also seem to suggest that, in the process involving the integration of Muslim immigrants into Canadian society, economic and social factors may be interrelated. How can this peculiar situation be ameliorated? This is the topic of the next chapter.

10

Solutions

How to Strengthen the Attachments of Muslims to Canada

The previous chapters show that the status of Muslims in Canada is visibly distinct from that of immigrants of other religious backgrounds. The data show that, while Muslims are generally satisfied with their lives in Canada, they tend to report a lower level of trust towards the general population, a lower level of life satisfaction, and a lower level of participation in electoral processes than do other immigrant groups. They also report an unusually high degree of concern about their future in Canada, about the likelihood of their experiencing discrimination and unemployment, and about the rise of extremism among Muslims. This mixed bag of findings implies that, as far as the place of Muslims in Canada is concerned, the current environment is reasonably acceptable but that this may change should the areas of concern be left unaddressed.

In trying to find the exact fault lines in the process of integrating Muslims into Canadian society, and in trying to identify the possible factors behind them, it is useful to distinguish between four main domains of integration: Canadian institutional space, the media, the economy, and the community. The evidence indicates no major problems in the first two domains but serious ones in the latter two. Furthermore, the latter two domains (the economy and the community) seem to be related. Our discussions in the previous chapters revealed that Muslims' difficulties in the economic domain could not be found in the quantity or quality of their human capital (e.g., educational credentials, language skills, and prior job experience). Rather, these

FIGURE 10.1
Predictors of attachment to Canada

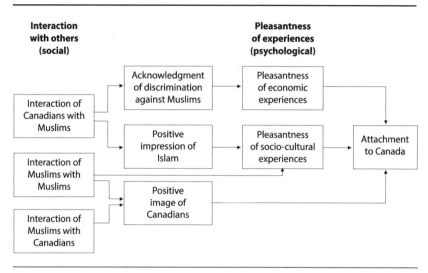

difficulties seem to have stemmed from the social elements of the economy (e.g., acceptance, discrimination, etc.). This is partially corroborated by the challenges Muslim immigrants face in the communal domain.

Making a distinction between the four different domains of integration helps us to better understand immigrant experiences as well as to make better policy. As I discuss in the next chapter, this approach enables us to analyze the different experiences of immigrants in different countries rather than to simply see this process as something universal and not context-dependent. And it allows for more focused policy interventions. Rather than spending valuable societal energy on all aspects and dimensions of integration, each country can focus on the areas that are most problematic.

My discussion in this chapter is guided by these three principles: (1) the social and economic areas of immigrant integration are the most challenging ones for Canadian Muslims; (2) improvements in these two domains would raise the level of Muslims' attachment to Canada; and (3) while the social and economic domains are interdependent, changes in the social domain influence the economic domain. The main tenets of these principles are presented in Figure 10.1.

The dependent variable in this conceptual framework is the strength of Muslims' attachment to Canada, measured through a variety of indicators, such as the strength of their sense of belonging to Canada, their trust of the general population, and their desire to adopt Canadian customs (as opposed to remaining culturally distinct). The independent variables are clustered under two broad headings: those related to the *pleasantness* of the experiences (both economic and social/cultural) and those related to the nature of *social interactions*. Below, in a series of hypotheses, I list the ways in which the independent variables affect the dependent variable.

- H1: *Pleasant economic experiences create a stronger attachment to Canada among Muslim immigrants.* The impact of economic experiences is particularly significant for immigrants as a large majority of them are, indeed, economic immigrants. However, as shown in Chapter 5, after the first four years of living in Canada, such experiences become paramount even for non-economic immigrants (such as family-class immigrants and refugees).
- H2: *The pleasantness of the socio-cultural environment creates a stronger attachment to Canada among Muslims.* Such pleasantness is the product of a range of experiences, such as the mainstream population and institutions displaying acceptance of the Muslim faith, thus allowing Muslims to express a strong sense of belonging to their own faith and cultural heritage without having to choose between that and Canada.
- H3: *An increased level of interaction between Muslims and native-born Canadians can result in a more positive and less stereotypical image of Canadians in the minds of Muslims and, in the process, can lead to a stronger attachment to Canada.*
- H4: *An increased level of interaction between native-born Canadians and Muslims will result in a more positive image of Islam and Muslims in the minds of Canadians; this more positive image will then contribute to the pleasantness of the socio-cultural environment for Muslims.* Increased interaction could lead to native-born Canadians' awareness of discrimination against Muslims in the job market. This could result in a decrease in the frequency of discriminatory behaviours and, in turn, increase the pleasantness of Muslims' economic experiences. This would generate a stronger sense of attachment to Canada. A more positive image of Islam in the minds of Canadians could also contribute to the pleasantness of Muslims' cultural experiences.
- H5: *An increase in the level of interaction among Muslims themselves can also result in an increased level of attachment to Canada.* This could come about through two different channels: (1) raising the pleasantness

of Muslims' cultural experiences with other Muslims and/or (2) raising Muslims' level of trust towards the general population among Muslims themselves. In other words, increasing the level of interaction between Muslims themselves will somehow result in a more positive and trusting view towards the non-Muslim general population.

I apply data from a variety of sources to these hypotheses. Some of these data are quantitative and come from nationwide surveys; some are qualitative and come from face-to-face interviews. While the qualitative data do not have the breadth and generalizability of the quantitative data, they do provide some empirical support for the theoretical possibilities suggested earlier and could well inform future research. Below, I assess the hypotheses in the order in which they were presented.

H1: *The pleasantness of economic experiences creates a stronger sense of attachment to Canada among Muslim Immigrants*

The overwhelming majority of Muslims in Canada are first- or second-generation immigrants, and a large proportion of them, like other immigrants, come to Canada in search of better economic conditions. For these immigrants, the quality of their economic experiences is one of the most influential factors in determining the level of their satisfaction with their migration experience and post-migration lives. As mentioned earlier, a general state of high satisfaction resulting from such experiences has the potential to lead to a stronger sense of attachment to Canada.

The psychological mechanism through which the nature of economic experiences could affect the sense of attachment to the host country may be described as follows. The pleasantness of immigrants' economic experiences creates a positive environment and warm feelings. And these positive feelings, in turn, inform the cognitive aspect of an immigrant's perception about his/her new country. As is the case in any situation in which an individual encounters a new environment, immigrants need to develop some type of understanding of their surroundings upon their arrival in the host country. Such an understanding is influenced not only by the quality of the information available to them but also, and perhaps much more so, by their emotional state. In other words, the appeal of a particular mode of understanding is less dependent on its accuracy in explaining realities than it is on its compatibility with someone's emotional state. Having pleasant economic experiences after migration could push immigrants towards having a more positive and optimistic explanation of how things work in their new homes

FIGURE 10.2

Muslims' overall satisfaction with the way things are going in Canada, by
their level of concern about unemployment among Muslim Canadians

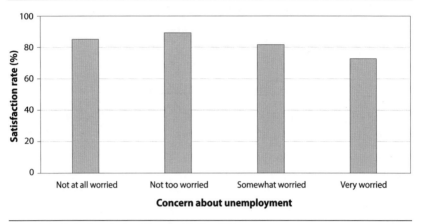

Source: Environics Institute, Survey of Canadian Muslims, 2006.

and, hence, towards developing a stronger sense of attachment to the new
society.

Figure 10.2 shows the possible connection between Muslims' level of
satisfaction with their post-migration lives and their concerns regarding the
likelihood of experiencing unemployment. While the graph shows that the
level of satisfaction is generally high – varying between 70 and 90 percent
– it also shows that, with the rise in the level of concern about Muslims'
unemployment, satisfaction levels start dropping. The difference between
the highest and lowest levels here is about 20 percent, which is significant.

The influence of economic concerns is not limited to life satisfaction.
Another, perhaps more important, consequence of such concerns may be
found in their impact on Muslims' concerns about their future in Canada.
Figure 10.3 shows that, with the increase in the level of concerns about unemployment, Muslims become noticeably more worried about their future
in Canada – with a more than 30 percent difference between the lowest and
the highest categories. This is an extremely important issue because optimism about the future often makes current problems more tolerable. When
the future looks bright, today's challenges tend to be viewed as temporary
and passing; when it does not, current problems tend to be seen as warning
signs of a similar or worse future.

FIGURE 10.3

Proportion of Canadian Muslims who are somewhat/very worried about their future in Canada, by their level of concern about unemployment among Muslim Canadians

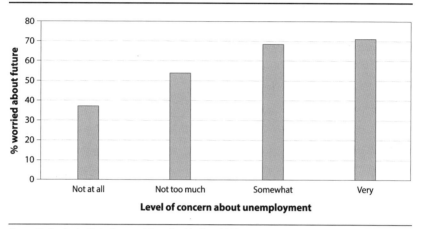

Source: Environics Institute, Survey of Canadian Muslims, 2006.

H2: *The pleasantness of socio-cultural experiences creates a stronger sense of attachment to Canada among Muslims*

In Chapter 8, I argue that the unique economic experiences of Muslim immigrants (i.e., their overrepresentation among the unemployed, the low-income, and so on) could not be easily explained by reference to their human capital. In Chapter 9, I suggest the possibility that those experiences could originate in the social component of the economic domain (i.e., the degree to which Muslims are accepted, and interacted with, by the mainstream population). This possibility is partially confirmed through the presence of a high level of concern among Muslims regarding discrimination. What gives such concern more credence is that it is expressed not only by Muslims themselves but also by native-born Canadians; and not only by native-born Canadians who have more sympathetic views of Muslims and more positive impressions of Islam but also by those who have a generally negative attitude towards Islam and Muslims.

The presence of possible discrimination against Muslims does not merely affect their economic performance, it can also directly affect their level of attachment to Canada. Figure 10.4 shows how the opinions of Muslims on a variety of issues are related to whether their experiences – due to their race, ethnicity, and/or religion – have been good or bad. The graph shows the

FIGURE 10.4

Responses of Muslim Canadians (who reported having had bad experiences
related to their race, ethnicity, and religion) to questions on some indicators
of attachment to Canada

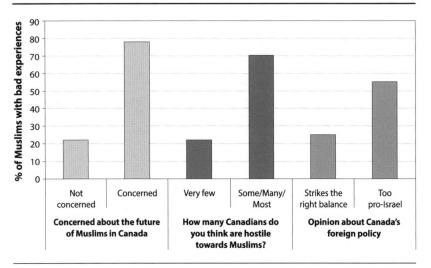

Source: Environics Institute, Survey of Canadian Muslims, 2006.

distribution of the responses of those who reported that they had bad experiences. These experiences seem to create not only a higher likelihood of
Muslims being concerned about their future in Canada but also a greater
percentage of those who think that native-born Canadians have a hostile
view towards Islam and Muslims.

Perhaps the most interesting feature of Figure 10.4 is the nature of the
responses to the question on Canadian foreign policy – that is, how pro-
Israel, pro-Arab, or balanced is it? Here again, the pattern remains the same:
those who have had bad experiences due to their culture, skin colour, and/
or religion consider Canadian foreign policy to be too pro-Israel. In other
words, the nature of Muslims' experiences in Canada appears to result in
opinions that go beyond the realities of their domestic lives.

The interesting relationship between the quality of experiences in Canada
and the opinions on Canadian foreign policy demonstrates that there is a
connection between emotional experiences and cognitive judgments. The
fact that those Muslims who have less than satisfying experiences inside
Canada are more likely to see Canadian foreign policy in the Middle East as
anti-Arab may imply that they view the treatment they receive in Canada as

part of a larger anti-Muslim bias. The extent of the influence of domestic experiences on views on foreign policy is about 20 percent (equivalent to the drop in the proportion of pro-Israel responses) when people switch from having bad experiences to having good ones.

The relationship between the nature of the treatment that Muslims receive from the host population and the strength of their positive views about Canada also surfaced in the interviews I conducted with Muslims in the course of this study. A male Pakistani immigrant in his thirties articulated this point by talking about how the openness of the host population had resulted in his having a stronger sense of identification with the Prairie city in which he lives:

> *Interviewer:* how do you feel about the city, the community, you
> live in?
>
> *Interviewee:* I think [the city's name] is one of the best cities in
> the world; and the reason is that people are very open – towards
> religion; people are very open towards new ideas; people are very
> friendly, they're very warm – despite the weather. There is in the
> city a lack of arrogance, which is good ... I don't associate myself
> [with] any [other] part of the world ... I feel more Canadian than
> I do anything else, for that matter.

Another Muslim immigrant, a Lebanese woman in her twenties who had lived in Canada for fewer than five years, expressed a similar view, pointing to the fact that Canadians' acceptance of diversity had driven her to explore her own identity more deeply and to develop a new identity in which "Canadian-ness" had a growing influence:

> I think people here like diversity. They like that whole diversity
> thing. Over there [in my home country], it's more, like, y'know:
> "being Lebanese is the best breed you can, we need to keep that
> pure race" ... And now I can feel I am closer and closer to identify-
> ing myself as Canadian Arab ... I feel that the longer I live here,
> the more I am accustomed to Canadian values, I accept a lot of it.
> And I feel that it can really be fused in with my Arab identity.

There are two key points that should be noted here. First, the develop-ment of a sense of belonging to Canada does not have to come at the expense of the immigrants' sense of belonging to their own ethnic/cultural heritage. As was shown before, an overwhelming majority of immigrants to this country combine a strong sense of belonging to Canada with an equally strong sense of belonging to their own ethnic/cultural group. This goes against the implications of the conventional assimilationist approach, in which the two senses of loyalties are treated as parts of a zero-sum game. Thus, it may be argued that the degree to which immigrants remain attached to their own ethnic/cultural heritage, as well as the degree to which this cultural loyalty is recognized, welcomed, and even celebrated in Canada, plays a crucial role in making their socio-cultural experiences in Canada pleasant.

The second point concerns the presence of a degree of interchangeability between the pleasantness of experiences in the socio-cultural domain and in the economic domain. Figure 10.5 shows the interplay between (1) the strength of a sense of belonging to one's ethnic/cultural group and to Canada and (2) the average income of immigrants. The respondents are all immigrants – not just Muslims – who have expressed a very strong sense of belonging to Canada but who have different levels of sense of belonging (strong and not strong) to their own ethnic groups. For each of these two groups, the average income is reported for the three waves of the LSIC survey (i.e., after six months, two years, and four years of living in Canada).

The interesting pattern in Figure 10.5 shows that those with a weaker sense of belonging to their own group have a noticeably higher average income than do those with a strong sense of attachment to their own group – a difference of about $10,000 annually. In other words, those with a stronger attachment to their own ethnic group seem to be more economically disadvantaged than do those with a weaker attachment. This particular pattern could be read and interpreted in several different ways, depending on one's perspective. One interpretation is that immigrants would be better off financially if they shed their attachment to their own ethnic/cultural group in favour of developing a strong sense of attachment to Canada. This is consistent with the assimilationist perspective and with the findings reported in Raza's (2012) study of immigrants' incomes.

One should, however, be cautious about the full implications of such an argument because the same study by Raza also shows that, while the assimilationists (i.e., those with a strong attachment to Canada and not to their own ethnic group) have higher incomes than the integrationists (i.e., those with a strong sense of belonging to both Canada and country of origin), an

FIGURE 10.5

Average income for those with a strong sense of belonging to Canada, by the strength of their sense of belonging to their own ethnic group

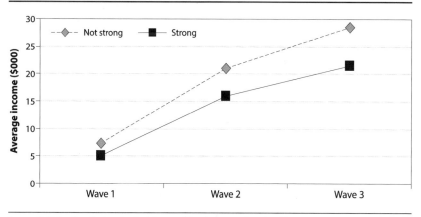

Source: Statistics Canada, Longitudinal Survey of Immigrants to Canada, 2005.

even higher income is earned by the so-called separationists (i.e., those who have a strong sense of belonging to their own ethnic group but not to Canada). And the highest income is reported by the individualizationists (i.e., those with a weak sense of belonging to both their own ethnic group and to Canada). In other words, if the income gap reported in Figure 10.5 is used as the basis of an argument in favour of assimilation, its logical extension would be an argument in favour of striving for no sense of belonging to any group, whether own ethnic group or Canada at large.

However, a more reasonable argument to make on the basis of the data presented in Figure 10.5 would be to strive for a degree of interchangeability between economic and social/cultural experiences. The fact that, despite an income difference of about $10,000, the two groups presented in this figure retain a strong sense of belonging to Canada suggests that, for immigrants who are economically disadvantaged, an attachment to own ethnic/cultural group serves as a shield against losing their sense of attachment to Canada. Thus, a reward in the job market and a recognition of the socio-cultural heritage of immigrants – both of which speak to the pleasantness of their post-migration experiences – go hand in hand to create a strong sense of belonging to Canada. This interchangeability is particularly relevant in the case of Muslims in Canada, given their consistent economic disadvantages.

H3: *An increased level of interaction between Muslims and native-born Canadians can result in a more positive and less stereotypical image of Canadians in the minds of the Muslims; this, in turn, can lead to a stronger sense of attachment to Canada among Canadian Muslims.*

The interaction between Muslims and native-born Canadians can occur in many different contexts – in the workplace, in schools, and in neighbourhoods. Among these, the relationships that occur in neighbourhoods are of particular importance as they are entirely voluntary and without the possible imposition of some impersonal forces such as work requirements or school policies. In other words, those who share a neighbourhood have the option of either living their lives independently from each other or in connection with each other. As a consequence, when such relationships exist, they are voluntary and, as a result, can exert a very strong influence not only on people's attitudes towards each other but also on their attitudes towards the larger society. Elsewhere, I show that receiving a favour from a neighbour raises the level of one's trust towards the society as a whole (Kazemipur 2009). Given the significance of neighbourhood dynamics, it would be useful to examine how they might influence Muslims' levels of attachment to Canada.

Figure 10.6 shows the distribution of immigrants with a strong sense of belonging to Canada across four categories: (1) those for whom the majority of neighbours are also newcomers to Canada, (2) those whose neighbours are predominantly native-born Canadians, (3) those who have friendly relationships with their neighbours, and (4) those who have unfriendly relationships with their neighbours. This categorization allows us to examine the relative impact of two features: (1) the diversity of the relationship (in terms of immigration status) and (2) the quality of the relationship (in terms of being friendly or unfriendly). The graph reports the data for Muslim immigrants and all other immigrants separately.

The two sets of bars – representing Muslim immigrants and all other immigrants – follow a similar general pattern. Consistent with the implications of hypothesis H3, the two groups that report the highest percentages of those with a strong sense of belonging to Canada are those that have friendly relationships with their neighbours, while those that report the lowest percentages have unfriendly relationships with their neighbours. So the pleasantness of the neighbourhood environment contributes to the strengthening of a sense of belonging to the country in general.

Focusing on the immigration status of those in shared neighbourhoods, we see that the respondents report a higher percentage of those who feel

FIGURE 10.6

Proportion of Muslims and other immigrants with a strong or very strong sense of belonging to Canada, by neighbourhood composition and relations

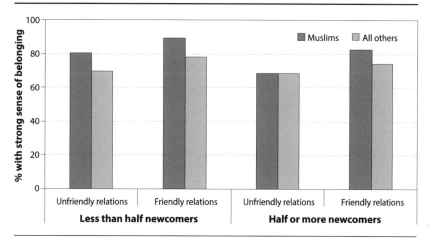

Source: Statistics Canada, Longitudinal Survey of Immigrants to Canada, 2005.

a sense of belonging to Canada when most of their neighbours are native-born Canadians. Interestingly enough, the same pattern holds even when they do not necessarily have friendly relationships with their native-born Canadian neighbours. This is a curious but interesting pattern. Why should an unfriendly relationship with native-born Canadian neighbours result in a higher percentage of people reporting a strong sense of belonging to Canada? The answer to this question requires some information beyond that provided by the data presented here. However, one may speculate that sharing a neighbourhood with native-born Canadians has the potential to give immigrants the feeling that they have been accepted into Canadian society rather than being segregated into predominantly immigrant enclaves. To see native-born Canadians living beside them in their neighbourhoods – which tend to be located in the lower-income zones of the cities – could create a sense of normalcy (as opposed to second-class citizenship) about their status in Canada.

The patterns in Figure 10.6 allow for a better understanding of the relative significance of two elements: (1) degree of pleasantness of experience and (2) interaction with native-born Canadians. In the category with the strongest sense of belonging to Canada, both elements are present: friendly relationship with mostly native-born Canadians. In the category with the smallest number, both elements are absent and, in their place, we have *un*friendly relationship with *non*-Canadians. The two categories in between are not as straightforward as the first two because each has a missing element. However, between these two, a higher percentage is reported for immigrants who have pleasant relationships with their mostly non-Canadian neighbours. This puts the pleasantness of experience slightly ahead of interaction with native-born Canadians in fostering a strong sense of belonging to Canada. Interestingly enough, the positive effect of the neighbourhood environment in creating a stronger attachment to Canada is even more pronounced for Muslim immigrants than it is for others.

The general similarity of the patterns for Muslims and all other immigrants, however, should not leave the impression that this is a universal phenomenon for immigrants of all religious backgrounds. An examination of the above pattern broken down by religious affiliation reveals, for instance, that Catholic immigrants deviate from this pattern in that their highest level of sense of belonging to Canada is reported when they live in the vicinity of other immigrants, regardless of whether they have friendly or unfriendly relationships with them. It is important to keep this distinction in mind because it shows that factors such as neighbourhood environment are context-dependent rather than universal. The differences between Catholic and Muslim immigrants in this regard, for instance, may be related to factors such as the different levels of diversity within each of these two groups, the ethnic composition of other immigrants with whom they share a neighbourhood, the population size of each group, and the nature of neighbourhood dynamics in countries of origin. An examination of the possible influences of these factors, however, falls beyond the scope of this study.

The exposure of Muslims to native-born Canadians raises the level of their attachment to and identification with Canada and Canadians. A similar process could work for Canadians as well: with an increase in the level of native-born Canadians' exposure to Muslims, there could be an increase in the former's level of comfort, trust, and sympathy with regard to the latter. I discuss this under hypothesis H4.

H4: *An increased level of interaction between native-born Canadians and Muslims will result in a more positive image of Islam and Muslims in the minds of Canadians.*

Figure 10.7 illustrates one possible consequence of increased contact between native-born Canadians and Muslims. It shows that, with an increase in the frequency of contact, native-born Canadians' impressions of Islam becomes increasingly positive. The strength of this correlation is so high

FIGURE 10.7
Proportion of native-born Canadians who have a positive impression of Islam, by their level of contacts with Muslims

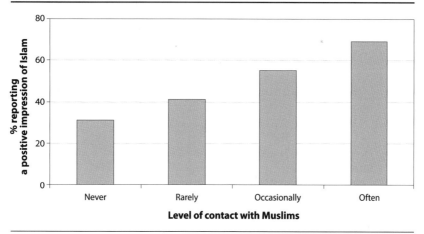

Source: Environics Institute, Survey of Canadian Muslims, 2006.

that, between those Canadians with no contact and those with frequent contact, there is an almost 40 percent difference in the percentages reported. It goes without saying that, if the native-born population had a more positive impression of Islam, the social and communal integration of Muslims would be much easier in many areas of social life (e.g., the workplace, school, and neighbourhoods).

Despite their close connection, however, one's impression of Islam and one's view of Muslims are two different things. These two measures may behave differently and may move in opposing directions. One simple reason for this is that, as with any faith community, the lifestyles of Muslims may not match the official instructions of their religion. The lifestyle of an individual Muslim immigrant could be influenced by a combination of forces: the official recommendations of her/his faith, the cultural tendencies of the country from which she/he has come, and her/his individual personality. This diversity of influences shows itself in the diversity of beliefs, practices, and lifestyles within Muslim populations.

So to what extent could one argue that increased frequency of contact with Muslims would result in a more positive image of Muslims in the minds of native-born Canadians? Unfortunately, the data used in this study do not include a question on Canadians' opinions about Muslims per se; however, there is a question regarding their opinions about Arabs. Despite the fact

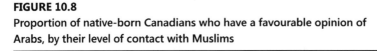

FIGURE 10.8

Proportion of native-born Canadians who have a favourable opinion of
Arabs, by their level of contact with Muslims

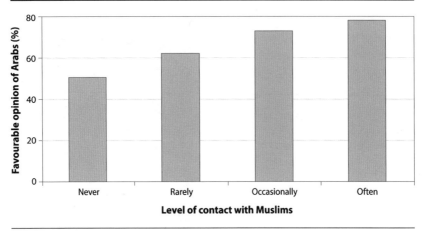

Source: Environics Institute, Survey of Canadian Muslims, 2006.

that Muslims should not be equated with Arabs, in the minds of many this
is exactly what occurs. Because of this, bearing the appropriate caveats in
mind, we can read the data on Arabs as data on Muslims.

Figure 10.8 shows that, with the increase in the level of contact with
Muslims, there is an increase in the proportion of native-born Canadians
who hold a favourable attitude towards Arabs. The strength of the trend is
quite noteworthy as, with every increase in the level of contact with Muslims,
there is a corresponding increase of about 10 percent for those who report
favourable opinions towards Arabs.

One particularly troubling finding discussed in the previous chapter
concerns the prevalence of discrimination against Muslims in Canada,
something that was reported almost to the same degree by both Canadian
Muslims and the native-born population. I suggested that the treatment
received in the job market and in the economic domain could be strongly
influenced by the presence of such discriminatory tendencies in Canadian
society. The obvious implication of this is that any improvement in the
economic status of Canadian Muslims would require a reduction in discrimination. An increase in the contact between Canadian Muslims and the
native-born population has the potential to remedy this problem.

Figure 10.9 shows the relationship between native-born Canadians' level
of contact with Muslims and their willingness to acknowledge that Muslims

FIGURE 10.9

Proportion of native-born Canadians who believe that Muslims are subjected to discrimination occasionally or often, by their level of contact with Muslims

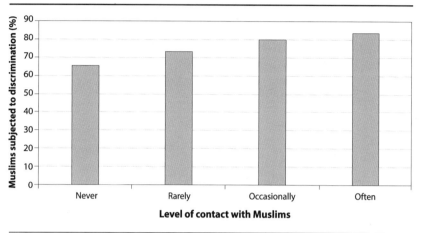

Source: Environics Institute, Survey of Canadian Muslims, 2006.

are subject to discrimination in Canadian society. Here again, with an increase in the frequency of contact, there is a corresponding increase in the proportion of those who are ready to admit that Muslims are subjected to discrimination occasionally or often. The difference in the percentages reported for the lowest and highest levels of contact is about 20 percent. Even among those Canadians with absolutely no contact with Muslims, about 65 percent admit that Muslims are frequently subjected to discrimination in Canadian society. Put side by side with a piece of information discussed in Chapter 9 – that is, Canadians, regardless of their positive or negative impressions of Islam, acknowledge discrimination against Muslims – Figure 10.9 reinforces the confidence in the data reporting the prevalence of discrimination against Muslims.

The positive impacts of contact and social interaction on inter-group attitudes are not unique to Muslims. What is unique to Muslims is the fact that native-born Canadians have a lower level of contact with them than they do with all other immigrant and non-immigrant groups – with more than 50 percent reporting their levels of contact with Muslims as being never or rarely. Thus, the benefits associated with such contact do not materialize for Muslims, simply because of low levels of contacts between them and native-born Canadians.

H5: *An increase in the level of interactions among Muslims themselves can also result in an increase in the strength of their attachment to Canada.*

The data provided under hypothesis H3 and hypothesis H4 show the two sides of one process: with Muslims' increased exposure to native-born Canadians, the former develops a more positive attitude towards the latter and vice versa. More interesting, and perhaps less intuitive, is the possibility that the increased exposure of Muslims to other Muslims results in a more positive attitude towards non-Muslims and a stronger attachment to Canada.

At least part of the reason that such a possibility may be considered counter-intuitive involves the implications of past research on social capital. Scholars in this field distinguish between "bonding" and "bridging" social capital, with the former referring to the connections among individuals of a similar background and the latter referring to the connections between those of different backgrounds. Many studies in this field emphasize the significance of bridging social capital for creating a sense of national solidarity, a smooth functioning democracy, and an efficient economic system. Bonding social capital, on the other hand, is associated with social fragmentation and premodern communal ties. The argument suggests that, in order for social solidarity to develop in today's modern and diverse societies, we need more bridging and less bonding social capital. However, what my hypotheses suggests is that, with more bonding social capital among Muslims, there could also be more bridging social capital between Muslims and non-Muslims.

Figure 10.10 provides some support for this. Reporting the relationship between Muslims' participation in religious services and their beliefs about Canadians' impression of Islam, this graph shows that, with an increase in the level of participation, a higher proportion of Muslims seem to develop a feeling that native-born Canadians view Islam in a generally positive light. Given the data presented earlier, such an impression has the potential to convince Muslims that Canadians do not have a generally hostile view towards them and, hence, that peaceful coexistence is possible.

A careful reader will see that the most noticeable increases occur in the middle zone; that is, in the medium-level participation range, peaking in the once-a-week category and slightly dropping afterwards. It could be argued that the amount of increase is not that noticeable and probably not statistically significant. This argument is well taken, but it does not undermine

FIGURE 10.10

Proportion of Canadian Muslims who believe that native-born Canadians have a positive impression of Islam, by frequency of their religious attendance

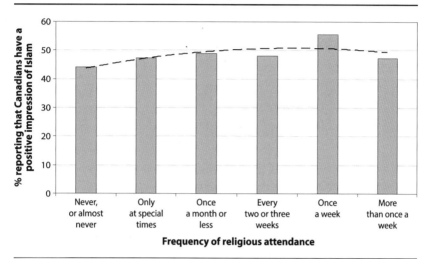

Source: Environics Institute, Survey of Canadian Muslims, 2006.

the generally rising nature of the trend. Even if one insists that the increase in positive attitudes should not be given too much weight, it is clear that the trend is not towards the negative, as previous research implies. And this, in and of itself, is an important finding. At the least, this figure confirms that the increased participation of Muslims in their faith-specific functions does not necessarily come at the expense of their connection to the broader population. Thus, a high level of interaction among Muslims should not automatically be viewed as part of a zero-sum balance with regard to their bond to the larger population.

A similar, but perhaps more convincing, piece of evidence may be found in the trends in Muslims' levels of trust towards the general population. As is highlighted in the social capital literature, the presence of a general trust in unknown others serves to lubricate the social and economic machinery, making cooperation and collaboration possible. It is therefore important to examine the extent to which such trusting views prevail among Muslims. Figure 10.11 reports the percentage of Muslims with a high trust in the general population according to their level of participation in religious services. The data show that a higher degree of attendance in religious functions generally leads to a higher level of trust. This is a finding that, again, is

FIGURE 10.11

Proportion of Canadian Muslims who totally agree that most people can be trusted, by frequency of religious attendance

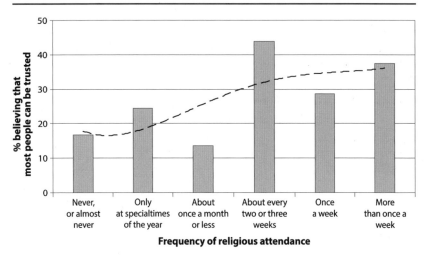

Frequency of religious attendance

Source: Environics Institute, Survey of Canadian Muslims, 2006.

contrary to social capital research, which suggests that an increase in bonding tends to weaken bridging.

How can exposure to people of similar background lead to more positive views towards people of different backgrounds? One explanation for the correlation between Muslims' participation in religious functions and their trust in the general population could be the increase in their exposure to diversity as a result of such participation. It is true that people attend religious functions primarily because of their shared beliefs; however, once contact is established with others, and particularly with others of different ethnic, national, or class backgrounds, various things can happen. For example, one's social scenery can be changed, and this can result in new connections – connections that could well be more human and personal than those established through the sharing of more formal and abstract religious beliefs. In an environment of collective activities and close interactions, it becomes very difficult to treat people according to demographic categories such as age, gender, religion, or nationality. Each person differs from the next, and each has to deal with the other's singularities. Also, in such environments, a variety of personalities, life histories, national backgrounds, ethnic/cultural heritages, and class affiliations is simultaneously at work. Further, different people may have different interpretations of shared religious principles. Religious beliefs enter into a complex and multi-layered web of relationships, thus becoming exposed to many other forces. As a consequence, these beliefs may undergo major transformations, opening up a space in which other people may be accepted despite their religious convictions. This is a process that Putnam and Campbell (2010, 532) refer to as the "spill-over" effect, whereby the radius of trust is extended to include even those people with whom one does not share beliefs or history.

Obviously, such a process is not merely a Muslim phenomenon: as Putnam and Campbell (2012) show, it can happen in any faith community. However, the process is especially relevant to Canadian Muslims as they make up a particularly diverse faith group when compared both to other immigrants in Canada and to Muslim communities in other immigrant-receiving countries. The diversity of Canada's Muslim population can be seen in the relatively high number of countries of origin for Muslim immigrants reported in the LSIC data. This diversity is in clear contrast not only to the composition of Muslims in many European countries, where Muslim populations have overwhelmingly come from only one or two relatively homogenous sources (e.g., Turks in Germany, North Africans in France, and South Asians in the United Kingdom), but also to the composition of immigrants of other religious backgrounds in Canada.

This spill-over effect is very interesting as it allows for two seemingly opposite forces – religious and secular – to come together. A process that starts with an immigrant's longing for community (a secular force) brings her/him to religion; the latter, in turn, leads to her/him expanding her/his views and radius of trust in order to incorporate people of other (or no) religious beliefs. In other words, the people who become more religious after migration also become more secular: they become more religious insofar as their faith is concerned and more secular insofar as the process through which they arrive at this faith is concerned. This is an extremely important dynamic: on the one hand, one becomes more religious through a secular force such as the emotional need for connection, and, on the other, one becomes more secular as a result of the process involved in embracing religion.

At first, this may sound paradoxical; however, one finds important precedents for the spill-over effect. Durkheim's analysis of religion is particularly helpful here. In his classic *On Suicide*, Durkheim (2006 [1897]) argues that, while Protestants are as devout and as religious as Catholics, the contents of the Protestant faith cover a smaller area of life than does the Catholic faith, leaving the rest to individual interpretation. That only a small area of life will be informed by religious principles is a defining feature of secularization. So the high level of Protestant devotion to faith (a religious force) comes with a small territory for religion (a secular force). Juxtaposing these two views, we can argue that an increased level of religiosity can be attributed to two different things: (1) a strong level of attachment to religion and (2) a dense web of religious instructions. Protestants are more religious as a result of the first dimension and less religious (i.e., more secular) as a result of the second.

By the same token, one may argue that the process of increased religiosity among Muslim immigrants could, simultaneously, involve both a religious element and a secular element. To put it another way, a major consequence of Muslims' involvement in collective religious functions is an increased volume of interaction with a diverse population – interaction that could well result in the development of new, broader, and more inclusive identities. Such identities would emphasize not only elements shared with other Muslims but also those shared with non-Muslims.

The survey data do not test this theory, but it did surface during face-to-face interviews. In particular, it seemed to resonate with the experiences of a Lebanese immigrant woman who had arrived in Canada in her teens. As a result of her increased interaction with Muslims from other Middle Eastern countries after her arrival, this woman adopted an increasingly religious view and lifestyle. This interaction transformed her previously exclusive Lebanese identity into a new and more inclusive Arab-Muslim identity, which was a direct reflection of the beliefs of the people with whom she started associating upon her arrival in Canada. But, more interestingly, these interactions with diverse Muslims resulted in a spill-over identification with non-Muslims. This fusion of identities became part of her vision for how she would like to raise her children, even should they decide to go back to her country of origin: "If my kids are growing up in a Lebanese society, I think I'd want them to learn the values that I've picked up from Canadian society and pass that on and then let them be who they want to be in a Lebanese society."

The process through which this woman developed her Muslim, Arab, and Canadian identity led her to entertain a much more universal and fluid identity for her children:

> I ... don't want my kids to have to be Arab-Muslim. Especially if
> I don't know who my future partner will be ... Assuming that this

partner is not going to be neither Arab, nor Muslim, then I have to
accommodate for the other party as well, because they're not [only
my children], right? Like, they're not only mine, right?"

We should keep in mind that this participant considers herself a devout
Muslim and feels strongly about her religion. However, her process of integration into Canadian society has been such that she feels no conflict between her own religious views and the clearly secular views involved with
transferring her "Canadian values" to her future children. She is even willing
to have her children's identity decided through a secular process of negotiation with her future partner.

To tie this immigrant's experience to our earlier discussion, we can map
out the process of her identity formation. First, a relatively secular, non-
practising female Muslim immigrant arrives in Canada from Lebanon.
Second, at school she finds herself in the company of other Muslim students who are neither Lebanese nor secular. Third, as a consequence of her
close friendship with these students, she develops a "united Arab-Muslim"
identity – an identity that she had not experienced in her native Lebanon.
Fourth, as a result of this experience, and also of the experience of living in
Canada, she finds her identity to be shifting more towards what she describes as a "Canadian-Arab" identity. Fifth, upon reflecting about her future family (partner and children), she is open to further broadening her
Canadian-Arab-Muslim identity to accommodate whatever identity her future partner might have. Her identity seems to have become open-ended
and universal. The various links in this identity chain – secular Lebanese,
Arab-Muslim, Arab-Canadian, and Arab-Canadian-universal – seem to be
in tandem with the nature and the composition of her current and/or future
social interactions.

A similar spill-over dynamic is found in the nature of the social network
of a male Muslim immigrant from Pakistan who is in this thirties and living
in the Prairies. He has a very positive view of his experience of migrating to
Canada and he also has a diverse social network. In response to a question
on the composition of his social network, he says:

> *Interviewee:* Most of my network is, I would say, community-
> based; I do have friends outside, but all of them are, most of them
> are friends because of the fact they are involved in some capacity
> with religion. I am [involved with] a multi-faith [initiative], so I
> know a lot of people from a lot of different religions ...

> *Interviewer:* What kind of people are these? From what religious
> backgrounds?"
>
> *Interviewee:* There are Hindus; there are Baha'is, Christians, Jews.
> Let's take the Jewish community. [They have] one of their biggest
> congregations here in [name of city]; our community is really good
> friends with them.

An interesting corollary to what this interviewee has to say is the fact that
exposure to such diverse religious and ethnic backgrounds has, on the one
hand, made categories such as ethnicity and religion less important in shaping relationships and, on the other, made individual characters more important as a basis for judging others. In response to a question regarding
why he associates with certain people, he says:

> One thing would be their characters; their characters play a major
> role in how we talk to each other ... [If you are asking me why I am
> friends with them] I don't know the answer to that. But, I like them;
> we hang [out] and kind of work together, and things work out.

Like the Lebanese immigrant woman, this Pakistani immigrant cares
deeply about his faith and is heavily involved in the affairs of his Muslim
community. However, at the same time, he has a strong sense of attachment to Canada and a great sense of openness towards other groups. These
two examples call into question the validity of the idea that belonging to a
particular ethnic/religious group and to Canada make for a zero-sum game;
rather, they show that there is, or that there can be, a positive correlation
between these two loyalties.

The empirical data discussed in this section suggest that, as far as identity and sense of belonging are concerned, the impact of one's exposure to
diversity can be threefold: (1) it can trigger a process of thinking about
one's own identity in ways not experienced before; (2) it can introduce
more flexibility regarding the contents of the identities to be acquired; and
(3) these contents can be strongly influenced by the nature of one's social
interaction with others. These dynamics challenge popular perceptions of
identity as a fixed and/or predetermined category and allows for a wider
range of outcomes.

Given these findings, I now turn to a discussion of the practical measures
that might be taken in order to strengthen the attachment of immigrants in

general, and Muslim immigrants in particular, to Canada. These suggestions might be helpful to public policy makers, community organizations, and even to those in the private sector. They are not meant to provide an exhaustive list of all possibilities; rather, they are meant to sensitize the reader to those possibilities hidden within existing programs. I also discuss the broader theoretical implications of my findings.

11
Conclusions and Implications

My main finding can be summarized as follows: the Muslim question is a product not of the teachings of Islam or of the fundamental beliefs of Muslims but, rather, of the particular sets of relationships between Muslims and others. The major implication of this finding is that we should shift our attention from the theological to the social. In other words, we should focus on bringing the social into current debates about Muslims, which, to this point, have centred on the theological. While related, the debate about Islam and the debate about Muslims are distinct, and neither should be reduced to the other.

This shift of attention from theology to the social implies that the solutions to various issues surrounding Muslims are more likely to be found in the realm of relationships, behaviours, and attitudes than in religious scripts. This should not be understood to suggest that there are no benefits in initiatives that focus on correcting ideas and removing misunderstandings both among and about Muslims; rather, it suggests that such initiatives are useful insofar as they facilitate social interactions but that they are not stand-alone solutions. Initiatives such as inter-faith dialogues and cultural awareness weeks will have only a limited impact if they are not supplemented with measures to increase the level of social interaction among people of different faiths.

Viewing the place of Muslims in Canada in a relational perspective, I propose that the encounter between Muslims and Canadian society occurs in four different domains: the institutional, the media, the economic, and the social. My findings suggest few to no major problems in the institutional and media domains. In other words, with some exceptions, there are no major biases against Muslims in the mandates and structures of Canadian public institutions or in the contents of the Canadian media. However, Muslims face major challenges in the economic and social domains. Furthermore, a big portion of the economic challenges seems to be related to the limited integration of Muslims into social spaces. Thus, improvements in the social domain could help in solving difficulties in the economic domain.

The adoption of a relational perspective, along with the findings of this study, has implications for at least two major current debates: (1) that on what constitute best practices with regard to the settlement and integration of immigrants in host societies and (2) that on multiculturalism, both in Canada and in other immigrant-receiving countries. Both these debates are currently being conducted by policy makers and academic researchers, although the former are more involved in concrete policies and programs and the latter are more involved in the philosophical foundations of such policies and programs. In the following pages, I review the implications of my findings for each of these two debates, following with a discussion of the implications for future research and a prediction of future trends.

Implications for Immigrant Integration Policies

There are already several programs and practices that comply with the principles cited above. One of these is the host family program, which is organized by immigrant services agencies and through which, upon arrival, a newcomer is matched with a volunteer family. The purpose behind such an arrangement is to ease the challenges and anxieties that immigrants face in their initial attempts to settle in Canada (i.e., preparation for a new climate, encounters with a new bureaucracy, language, culture, job market, etc.). Those immigrants who are fortunate enough to be offered a host family readily admit to the huge weight lifted from their minds with regard to their immediate post-migration settlement.

One problem with the existing program, however, is that it is designed to help with immediate problems only – that is, with short-term and mostly bureaucratic problems. That is why the agencies in charge of this kind of program welcome any host family and/or individual who may volunteer to help, regardless of whether or not they are from an ethnic/national background similar to that of the arriving immigrant. The problem with this approach is that, when both the landing and hosting individuals and/or families are of the same ethnic background, while the arrangement serves to ease the immediate settlement pressures, it does little to foster social ties between immigrants and native-born Canadians. In order to be more strongly aligned with the findings of this study, host family programs need to be fine-tuned so as to maximize the chances of interaction between immigrants and the mainstream population. In the friendly and collaborative environment created by these kinds of programs, it is likely that both parties will develop more positive attitudes towards one another.

Educational settings are another environment in which one will find many opportunities for interaction between newcomers and the mainstream population. The natural increase in the diversity of the Canadian population is clearly reflected in the schoolyard and the classroom, and this obviously increases the probability of interaction between students of different backgrounds. However, given the implications of contact theory, such interactions are most constructive and effective when they occur within a neutral environment in which students collaborate towards achieving a common goal. If they are aware of this principle, teachers can try to maximize the diversity of a group's student body before working on a team project rather than leaving it to chance or to student preferences (something that could generate the opposite outcome).

In addition to host population and institutions, minorities and immigrants themselves could benefit from my findings in fine-turning their initiatives. Consider, for example, the establishment of minority-only educational institutions (such as Islamic or black-only schools). The main idea behind initiatives such as this is that, through exposure to culturally specific curricula, students will have an opportunity to learn more about their own cultural heritages. This is a noble idea; however, in its extreme form it can rob students – both majority and minority students – of the opportunity to interact with people of different cultural backgrounds. In such a case, the ability of such schools to provide children with chances to develop a common identity with their fellow citizens would be fairly limited.

When immigrant children attend only their own special schools, the outcome is individuals who are uni-culturally aware but socially isolated. And this leads to a fragmented society. However, this should not be taken as an argument against establishing minority-only schools. Given the fact that such schools come in many different forms – from full-time and all-week to part-time and after-hours or weekend schools – their impact varies greatly. In principle, however, the promoters of such schools should bear in mind that a better awareness of one's cultural heritage does not have to come at the expense of one's ability to work and live side by side with people of different ethnic and cultural backgrounds. After all, it is only when they create the atmosphere of the outside world that minority-only schools can help prepare children to enter that world. Therefore, it would be better for such schools to combine an awareness of one's cultural heritage with a high level of social interaction with those who belong to different cultural and ethnic groups.

Another area that could benefit from my findings concerns the distribution of minority and immigrant populations in urban residential space. To be sure, the bulk of the decisions about where to live are made on the basis of socio-economic considerations. However, there are situations in which other considerations come into play, such as when governments try to decide where to house government-assisted refugees or when immigrants decide to create culturally specific neighbourhoods. In such situations, decisions should take into account the implications of my study. In the case of public housing projects, for instance, decisions should be made with an eye to maximizing social diversity as opposed to creating an environment in which low-income immigrants meet only other low-income immigrants. Similarly, decisions on building cultural centres should take into consideration maximizing the interaction of people of different backgrounds. A recent example of this surfaced in the discussions in Calgary after the official opening of the Baitunnur Mosque in 2007. Some Muslims expressed interest in making the mosque an architectural centre for a big Muslim neighbourhood and business centre. While this idea would certainly have made life much easier for Muslims, allowing them to live in a small semi-independent segment of the urban space, it would also have minimized their interaction with the larger population. The only outcome of such an initiative would have been the reinforcement of sectarian identities among Muslims and the continuation of anti-Muslim stereotypes in the mainstream population.

Based on the idea of maximizing interaction with different others, the preceding suggestions add a new element to the current understanding of inter-group relations. As things stand now, this understanding is geared towards raising cultural awareness. In the case of Muslims, such efforts aim at introducing a gentler, more peaceful, and more compromising version of Islam – one that differs from the extremist versions that currently receive most of the media attention. For the most part, the essence of such efforts is one-way education. Others take this a step further and call for two-way education (i.e., they encourage the exchange of information through face-to-face conversations). The following quote from a male Muslim immigrant in his thirties who is living in the Prairies and making an effort to improve the relationship between Muslims and native-born Canadians in his community illustrates this mode of understanding:

> Wherever I go, I personally want people to know that I am a Muslim ... My kids are the same way. Wherever we go, if it is a new place, we try to let people know somehow that we are Muslim. And we use that in a positive way, because if they are comfortable with you, and then they know that you are Muslim as well, then they will ask you questions. And that process of dialogue is what we look for because that is how we are going to get out of the stereotypical issues, right?

While the dialogical approach is one step ahead of one-way education, it still suffers from viewing a shortage of information as the main problem. As a result, the two-way exchange of information falls short of suggesting, or creating the right environment for, social interaction. An approach informed by the principle of maximizing social interaction would go beyond creating an information-sharing environment towards one that promotes openness, tolerance, sympathy, and the dismantling of stereotypes. It would help to generate the right milieu for the development of emotional bonds and common identities.

In order for this to happen, cognitive exchanges need to be augmented by the promotion of social interaction. Muslim minorities need to engage with the mainstream population in neighbourhoods, workplaces, schools, clubs, voluntary associations, and charity organizations. Through such interaction, they can remove uncertainties about Muslims in the minds of their non-Muslim fellow citizens. The improvements made in the social domain will then have the potential to make things more smooth in the job market and, in the process, improve the treatment and opportunities afforded to Muslims.

Besides having implications for immigrant integration programs and practices, my findings may also be used to inform the philosophical foundation of such macro-state policies as multiculturalism. Given the central place of Muslims in the current debates on multiculturalism policies, and the prominence of multiculturalism in Canada, it is appropriate to look at how this study might affect the broader debate in this area.

The Implications for the Multiculturalism Debate

As discussed in Part 1, the presence of Muslims in many Western liberal democracies is increasingly viewed as a challenge to the concept and policies of multiculturalism. The main reason for this view is twofold and has been popularized and reinforced by the mainstream media: (1) Muslims' beliefs involve a series of illiberal values, and (2) the recognition of those values through multiculturalism policies may provide them with a legitimacy and social space that they should not have within a liberal democracy. In this view, the main source of tension between Muslims and liberal democracies is the disagreement over the three fundamental principles of liberal democracies: freedom, equality, and solidarity.

The evidence for the uneasy relationship between the Islamic faith and freedom, the first core value of liberal democracies, is found in the occasional eruption of Muslim protest over certain cultural and artistic products. Consider, for example, the objections of Muslims, in both Muslim and non-Muslim countries, to the publication of Salman Rushdie's *The Satanic Verses* back in 1989. Since then there have been similar occasions, including the angry reactions of Muslims to the publication of cartoons of Muhammad in the Danish press (2005), the worldwide protests condemning the threat by Terry Jones (a Florida-based pastor) to burn the Quran (2010), the violent demonstrations against the producers of the anti-Muslim film *The Innocence of Muslims* (2012), and, most recently, the publication of the so-called French cartoons (2012). According to some critics of multiculturalism, honouring the demands of such protestors would effectively undermine freedom of expression.

Equality, the second core value of liberal democracy, is also sometimes seen as being in conflict with certain Islamic beliefs. In Canada, for instance, the negative reaction to the establishment of Sharia-based arbitration courts in Ontario and the outcry over practices such as "honour killing" were partly fed by the concern that multiculturalism would make it easier for Muslim communities to undermine the equality of women. The sociopolitical crisis in Quebec between 2005 and 2007 around the issue of reasonable accommodation had similar concerns at its heart.

Critics view the concept of *ummah* – the global Muslim community – as undermining solidarity, the third core value of liberal democracy. A commitment to a global community, the argument goes, comes at the expense of loyalty to nation-states, and this can threaten the stability of liberal democracies, which are primarily nation-states. For these critics, it was because of their commitment to *ummah* that the eighteen terrorist suspects of

Muslim background who were arrested in Ontario lacked loyalty to Canada. Given the centrality of the concept of *ummah* in Islam, the tension between Muslims and liberal democracies is sometimes viewed as impossible to resolve.

It is not difficult to imagine why those who believe in a fundamental conflict between the Islamic faith and the main principles of liberal democracy are also critical of multiculturalism. In their view, multiculturalism provides protection for the illiberal beliefs of Muslims and, hence, reinforces a major conflict between Muslims and liberal democracies. In response, proponents of multiculturalism make great efforts to resolve this conflict. Most of these efforts, however, are made in the form of philosophical and/or legal recommendations. In most cases, the two reinforce each other as philosophical principles are often used to inform the legal processes. To be sure, these contributions have been helpful in settling some special and particularly high-profile cases in the court system, but they fall short of providing a more enduring framework for resolving fundamental issues. This is because philosophical-legal frameworks are too static, abstract, and short-term. I would argue that our understanding of the apparent conflict between Islam and liberal democracies could benefit greatly from the adoption of a sociological perspective – one that takes into account the dynamics of inter-group relationships (for examples of this, see Kazemipur 2009; Reitz et al. 2009).

The first step in the shift from a philosophical-legalistic to a sociological perspective on the Muslim question involves the need to rethink freedom, equality, and solidarity not only as the philosophical underpinnings of liberal democracy but also as real social forces. From this perspective, we need to pay attention to how the social forces attached to each of these three values *actually* and *empirically* work. As the history of liberal democracies has shown, these three principles may not always work in harmony and, from time to time, may enter into conflict with one another. One way to resolve such conflicts is to explore how things might be reconceptualized so as to remove the points of tension; another way is to think about the social effects of such conflicts and their significance for the functioning of society. It is in the latter sense that a sociological approach is useful.

From a sociological perspective, one may ask a different set of questions than may be asked from a philosophical-legal perspective. For instance, one may ask whether a commitment to equality can materialize in the absence of a minimum degree of social cohesion and solidarity. Or whether solidarity can be promoted without equality. Or whether freedom can be promoted

FIGURE 11.1

Two sequencing orders for core liberal-democratic values

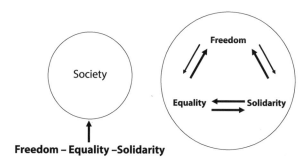

in the absence of equality. Asking such questions shifts the attention away from possible logical inconsistencies among and between freedom, equality, and solidarity and towards how they work in the real world.

Focusing on the empirical behaviours and/or the social forces associated with these core liberal-democratic values, I argue that there is a causal sequence between them. In other words, the full actualization and proper functioning of these values is contingent upon the presence of others. My understanding of this empirical behaviour informs the alternative conceptual arrangement that I suggest in Figure 11.1. Rather than setting all these values horizontally and so presenting them as having an assumed equal footing in reality – which seems to be the current view of liberal political philosophers – I present them in a triangular shape, with equality and solidarity residing at the bottom and freedom residing at the top. The arrows in Figure 11.1 indicate the presence of mutual influences; however, these influences are not equal in magnitude and strength.

It is important to keep in mind that I am not promoting these three values in different degrees; rather, I am offering a conceptual scheme of the extent to which each of them is dependent upon the other. The benefit of this scheme is that it gives policy makers and community activists a guideline that they may use in order to focus their energy more effectively.

How does this perspective help with the issues raised in the debates over Muslims and multiculturalism? So far, the bulk of the concerns about the unsuitability of Muslims for life in liberal democracies has been concentrated around the principle of freedom and, to a lesser extent, the principle of solidarity. Accordingly, remedial efforts have also concentrated on how minority rights could be reconciled with the principle of freedom so that the outcome would see Muslims living a peaceful life in non-Muslim liberal democracies. An implicit assumption of these remedial efforts is that, by focusing on and dealing with the problems associated with the principle of freedom, all the problems associated with Muslims and multiculturalism can be resolved. I, however, suggest that the tensions around the principle of freedom are unlikely to significantly subside without providing an equal focus on the problems associated with the principles of equality and solidarity.

I would therefore suggest that more attention be paid to Muslims' economic experiences (as a way to promote equality) and also to the level of their social contact with the mainstream population (as a way of strengthening solidarity). The measures taken in the economic realm will address the problem of inequality that Muslims seem to be currently experiencing in the Canadian job market. The increased social contact with the mainstream population will mutually reinforce the sense of attachment between the two groups and will result in a shared sense of solidarity. With improvements in these two areas, the need to use freedom will subside and be limited to expressing oneself, as opposed to fixing major structural problems in the social and economic domains. This does not mean that there will be any restrictions on freedom; rather, it means that concerns about the violation of such freedoms will subside. The forums in which freedom of expression is debated will no longer be the main battlegrounds for structural social and economic justice.

The shift from a philosophical-legalistic to a sociological perspective on the Muslim question has a second component, which involves viewing the issue as dynamic and historically based rather than as static and decontextualized. This approach draws attention to two related areas: (1) possible changes in the situations of minority groups who, in the past, may have been in a similar situation to that which Muslims are experiencing today, and (2) new intellectual developments in the Muslim world whose goal is to provide an interpretation of Islam that is more democracy-friendly. These two sets of developments have far-reaching implications for the ways in which the Muslim question might be understood.

It is also important to remember that the challenges that Muslim immigrants face today are not without precedent. In the past there have been many other immigrant groups whose integration into receiving societies was seen as dubious and unlikely and who nevertheless managed to integrate successfully. Lucassen (2005) documents the experiences of a few such groups, including Irish immigrants in Britain (1840-1922), Poles in Germany (1870-1940), and Italians in France (1870-1940). In all of these cases, the immigrants were primarily viewed as a threat either to the economy, to the security, or to the national identity of the host society. Such concerns, however, dissipated over time, and more balanced relationships were developed between the native-born populations and the immigrants, particularly those in the second and third generations.

The experiences of Irish immigrants in Britain are particularly relevant to this study. While in the case of other immigrant groups political and economic concerns were dominant, in the case of Irish immigrants the complicating factor was religion. As Lucassen (2005, 29) reports, Anglican and Protestant British perceived Roman Catholicism "to be a dangerous religion." In addition, the involvement of some of these immigrants in secret societies whose goal was to mobilize Irish immigrants in support of an independent Ireland made the majority of English citizens even more suspicious of them. Comparing these immigrants and Muslim immigrants today, Lucassen argues that "the gap between [Catholic Irish immigrants and the Anglican/Protestant English] was even deeper than that which exists between Christians (and agnostic western Europeans) and Muslims at the present time" (48). The integration of Irish immigrants and their younger generations into predominantly Protestant nations bears little resemblance to their initial experiences.

Another story of successful integration is that of Jewish minorities. Reporting the findings of a study of religion in the United States, Putnam and Campbell (2010) show that, when American respondents were asked about their feelings towards people of other religious groups, the warmest feelings were for Jews, mainline Protestants, and Catholics. They acknowledge that the finding with regard to Jews is likely the most surprising for some readers, "given the past intensity of anti-Semitism both in the United States and abroad" (506); however, they argue that this should not really be surprising because anti-Semitic sentiments in the United States have been falling since the end of the Second World War. In other words, the warmth of the relationships between, and the strength of positive feelings towards, members of different faith communities has undergone major transformations without any accompanying changes in religious scriptures or teachings.

A third example of successful integration, which is both more recent and more relevant to Muslims, involves the fact that some Islam sects – such as Ismailis and Ahmadis – have managed to combine a commitment to their faith with life in modern society. While there are theological debates within the broader Muslim community regarding the degree of compliance between the beliefs of these particular sects and "authentic Islam," they are nevertheless committed to their often very conservative beliefs. The fact that those beliefs have not prevented them from fully participating in the modern life of immigrant-receiving industrial countries serves to confirm the possibility of living a life that is loyal both to the Islamic faith and to liberal-democratic principles (see Daftary 2011; Gualtieri 2004; Karim 2011).

The shift in the position of the above groups – Catholics, Jews, and Ismaili and Ahmadi Muslims – towards a peaceful coexistence with the mainstream populations in Western countries has not occurred in a vacuum. Indeed, as a result of engagement with the world outside their faith communities, these groups developed new interpretations of their beliefs – interpretations that were more compatible with the three basic principles of liberal democracies. McGreevy (2003), for instance, offers a detailed historical account of the intellectual process through which Catholics constantly reinterpreted their social and political philosophy until it became more receptive to the ideas of freedom, equality, and democracy. McGreevy's account demonstrates the long and complicated nature of this process, and it clearly shows that, without the heavy engagement of Catholics with the outside world and vice versa, such a transformation would not have been possible.

Intellectual developments similar to those that have taken place within Roman Catholicism are also happening among Muslims. Over the past two decades, an increasing number of Muslim scholars have begun advocating for a fresh look at Islamic principles in the context of life in a liberal democracy. The conceptual underpinning of these intellectual contributions could be summarized as an effort to bridge the gap between Islam and concepts such as respect for human rights, individualism, democracy, pluralism, and tolerance (for a brief introduction to some of these contributions, see, among others, Abu-Zayd 2004; Arkoun 1994; Ramadan 2002, 2010; Soroush 2002). A discussion of the specific contents of these intellectual developments is beyond the scope of this book, but it is necessary to draw attention to something that all of these thinkers have in common: their recognition of the need for a more democratic interpretation of their faith emerged from, or was significantly reinforced by, their exposure to life in liberal democracies. Genuine engagement with liberal democracies, and becoming aware of their benefits, seems to have formed the intellectual foundation for these thinkers. In other words, interaction with the other is instrumental in the process of Islam's coming to terms with liberal democracies.

The Future?

As risky a business as it might be, I conclude with a word or two about the future of Muslims in Canada and elsewhere, and the future of research on Muslims. What I have to say about the future should be taken not as a prediction but as a framework within which to monitor developments, to talk about possible paths, and to learn about the forces at work.

What is fundamentally at issue here is the relationship between two groups: Muslims and native-born populations. While many factors shape such a relationship, and while inter-group relationships have their ups and downs, existing scholarship points to a pattern in the lifecycle of this relationship. This pattern is informed by a long tradition of research on neighbourhood dynamics, particularly in the United States; however, the findings may also be used with regard to cities, provinces, and countries. Figure 11.2 indicates various phases in the process of forming inter-group relationships at the neighbourhood level.

The pattern in Figure 11.2 concerns the changes in the level of social comfort of the majority group as a result of an increase in the population of a

FIGURE 11.2

Minority population and inter-group relationships at neighbourhood level

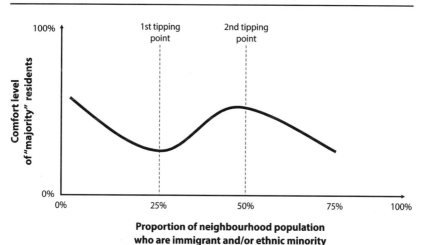

minority group in a neighborhood. The pattern highlights two tipping points (Sigelman et al. 1996; Kanter 1977; Blalock 1967) in the social climate. What the figure shows is that, when the population of a neighbourhood's minority group reaches the 20 to 30 percent level, it triggers a positive shift in the attitudes of other residents towards that group. Later, as this figure approaches the 50 to 60 percent threshold, there is a change in the opposite direction. The presence of these two tipping points results in three phases (shown as three zones in Figure 11.2) involved in this process of forming neighbourhood inter-group relationships.

In the first phase, the comfort level of the majority declines, primarily as a result of unexpected changes in the social scenery resulting from the entrance of "strangers." The sudden appearance of those strangers, especially if it occurs quickly, leads the majority to ask who these people are, where they have come from, what kind of lifestyle they have, how one should approach them, what constitutes acceptable and unacceptable norms of interaction, and so on. The lack of answers to such a wide range of questions has the potential to turn the social landscape into a less familiar zone, and this can result in mental strain among the initial residents. In such an environment, the decline in the majority group's emotional comfort and the development of negative attitudes towards the minority group becomes more likely. The decline in the comfort level in this phase is due to a combination of two forces: (1) the presence of strangers, which generates new questions for the majority, and (2) the small size of the minority, which does not allow for adequate interaction with the majority and, consequently, ensures that the latter's questions are left unanswered. Thus, in this phase, the majority group's attitudes towards the minority group are shaped by demographic changes in combination with the absence of social interaction.

The second phase is marked by an increase in the comfort level of the majority as social interaction is added to the picture. This occurs because a continuing increase in the population of the minority creates more opportunities for social interaction between the two groups. Such contacts often lead to the shattering of stereotypes on both sides and to the development of less biased views and more friendly relationships. So in the second phase (when the population of the minority approaches the 50 percent mark) the social contact component becomes the determining factor, overwriting the negative impact of the change in the neighbourhood's demographic landscape.

In the third phase (when the population of the minority passes the 50 percent mark), yet another element enters the scene. In this situation, in terms of sheer population size, the minority simply becomes the new majority, and this can easily lead to the old majority feeling as though its neighbourhood has been taken over. This can trigger a sense of threat and, consequently, may result in a decline in the level of comfort the majority feels in its relationship with the minority.

These neighbourhood dynamics could also occur in cities, provinces, and countries. Some examples of this include: in Vancouver, the initial negative reaction to the influx of immigrants from Hong Kong and the subsequent decline of these negative feelings; in Quebec, the negative reaction of Quebeckers to Muslim immigrants and its subsequent decline; and so on.

The three phases involved in forming neigbourhood inter-group relations do not surface in a neat sequence, nor do they surface solely in response to demographic change. Indeed, the duration of each of them will vary, depending on the impact of at least four other forces: (1) the rate at which the minority population increases, (2) the initial homogeneity of the majority population, (3) the economic environment, and (4) the entrance status of immigrants. In terms of the consequences for inter-group relations, the worst possible combination of these factors occurs when a minority's population rises at a very fast rate, the majority population is relatively homogeneous, there is an economic downturn, and the immigrants entering the local and social structure are of high status. The presence of such forces makes the second phase – the only phase marked with a positive social environment and healthy inter-group relationships – incredibly short.

In the case of Muslims in Canada today, three of the above four forces are working against the development of a positive inter-group relationship. The population of Muslims in Canada has been increasing quickly, the economic environment has not been very favourable, and a large number of Muslim immigrants are professionals who were selected via the point system to fill positions high up on the occupational ladder. On the other hand, the relative heterogeneity of the Canadian population makes it more receptive to new groups. One must also consider the influence of the popular media, which could make the "fear element" of the third phase enter the scene prematurely.

The relationship between Muslims and native-born Canadians shows signs of being in the first phase, with some small forays into the second phase. Where the environment is favourable for a majority backlash against Muslims, some right-wing circles with explicit or implicit anti-Muslim biases seem to be pushing society to skip the second phase altogether and go straight to the third. For the proponents of inclusive citizenship, the task should be to push the relationship between mainstream society and Muslims into the second phase and keep it there. I contend that this is possible in Canada through a commitment to equality for Muslims and through the promotion of social interactions between them and the rest of the population. In order for this to happen, the mainstream population and institutions need to genuinely engage with Muslims, and Muslims need to view Canada as their home – as opposed to a temporary place of residence – with all the associated rights and responsibilities that this entails. Unless some violent/terrorist incident stirs emotional responses and disturbs the normal course of events beyond repair, I predict that this mutual engagement is what is most likely to occur in Canada.

Needless to say, no single study could or should claim to have the final word in any research domain, and this one is no exception. If anything, my findings indicate areas that deserve further exploration. These include: the experiences of second-generation Muslim immigrants; the diversity of experiences within the Muslim population (based on national origin, sectarian affiliations, language, immigration class, and gender); international differences with regard to those experiences (e.g., Europe, the United States, and Canada); intellectual developments among Muslim scholars who are generating interpretations of Islam that are more compatible with pluralism, individualism, and democracy; and, finally, a more thorough understanding of the nature and dynamics of religiosity, secularism, and secularization among Muslims.

References

Abu-Zayd, N. 2004. *Reformation of Islmaic Thought: A Critical Historical Analysis.* Amsterdam: Amsterdam University Press.

Ahmed, A. 2010. *Journey into America: The Challenge of Islam.* Washington, DC: Brookings Institution Press.

al-Gharzawi, Y. 2005. *On Jurisprudence of Muslim Minorities: Lives of Muslims in Non-Muslim Societies* [Fi fiqh al-aqalliyyat: Hayat el-Moslemin vasat al-mojtama'at al-okhra]. Cairo: Dar-al-shorough.

Ali, A. 2007. "A Case of Mistaken Identity: Inside and Outside the Muslim Ummah." In N. Bakht, ed., *Belonging and Banishment: Being Muslim in Canada*, 99-104. Toronto: TSAR Publications.

Allport, G. 1979 [1954]. *The Nature of Prejudice.* 25th Anniversary Edition, Reading, MA: Addison-Wesley.

Arat-Koc, S. 2006. "Whose Transnationalism? Canada, 'Clash of Civilizations' Discourse, and Arab and Muslim Canadians." In V. Satzewich and L. Wong, eds., *Transnational Identities and Practices in Canada*, 216-40. Vancouver: UBC Press.

Archer, M.S. 1996. *Culture and Agency: The Place of Culture in Social Theory.* Cambridge: Cambridge University Press.

–. 2001. *Being Human: The Problem of Agency.* Cambridge: Cambridge University Press.

Arkoun, M. 1994. *Rethinking Islam: Common Questions, Uncommon Answers.* Boulder, CO: Westview Press.

Babul, A. 2008. "Knowing the Universe in All Its Conditions." In N. Bakht, ed., *Belonging and Banishment: Being Muslim in Canada*, 26-42. Toronto: TSAR Publication.

Bakht, N. 2007. "Religious Arbitration in Canada: Protecting Women by Protecting Them from Religion." *Canadian Journal of Women and Law* 19(1): 119-44.

–. 2008a. "Victim or Aggresssor? Typecasting Muslim Women for Their Attire." In N. Bakht, ed., *Belonging and Banishment: Being Muslim in Canada*, 105-13. Toronto: TSAR Publications.

–, ed. 2008b. *Belonging and Banishment: Being Muslim in Canada.* Toronto: TSAR Publications.

Banting, K., and W. Kymlicka, W. 2004. "Canada, Not America." *Prospect,* March.

Berger, P.L. 1967. *The Sacred Canopy: Elements of a Sociological Theory of Religion.* Garden City, NY: Doubleday.

Blalock, H.M. 1967. *Toward a Theory of Minority-Group Relations.* New York: Wiley.

Blume, L.E., and D. Easley. 2008. "Rationality." In S. Durlauf and L.E. Blume, eds., *The New Palgrave Dictionary of Economics.* 2nd ed. New York: Palgrave Macmillan.

Borjas, G.J. 1994. "The Economics of Immigration." *Journal of Economic Literature* 32: 1667-717.

Bouchard, G., and C. Taylor. 2008. *Building the Future: A Time for Reconciliation.* Complete report. Québec: Commission de consultation sur les pratiques d'accomodement reliées aux différences culturelles.

Bourdieu, P. 1979. *Algeria 1960.* Trans. R. Nice. Cambridge: Cambridge University Press.

–. 1984. *Distinction: A Social Critique of the Judgement of Taste.* Trans. R. Nice. Cambridge: Harvard University Press.

–. 1993. *Sociology in Question.* Trans. R. Nice. Thousand Oaks, CA: Sage.

–. 2005. *The Social Structure of the Economy.* Trans. C. Turner. Cambridge: Polity.

Bourdieu, P., and J.S. Coleman, eds. 1991. *Social Theory for a Changing Society.* Boulder, CO: Westview Press.

Burt, R.S. 1995. *Structural Holes: The Social Structure of Competition.* Cambridge: Harvard University Press.

Callero, P.L. 2003. "The Sociology of the Self." *Annual Review of Sociology* 29(1): 115-33.

Carliner, G. 1980. "Wages, Earnings and Hours of First, Second and Third Generation American Males." *Economic Inquiry* 18(1): 87-102.

Cerulo, K.A. 1997. "Identity Construction: New Issues, New Directions." *Annual Review of Sociology* 23(1): 385-409.

Cesari, J. 2005. "Islam, Secularisim and Multicutluralism after 9/11: A Transatlantic Comparison." In J. Cesari and S. McLoughlin, eds., *European Muslims and the Secular State,* 39-54. Burlington, VT: Ashgate.

Cliteur, P. 2010. *The Secular Outlook: In Defense of Moral and Political Secularism.* Malden, MA: Wiley-Blackwell.

Coleman, J. 1990. *Foundations of Social Theory.* Cambridge: Harvard University Press.

Costa, D.L., and M.E. Kahn. 2003a. "Civic Engagement and Community Heterogeneity: An Economist's Perspective." *Perspectives on Politics* 1(1): 103-11.

–. 2003b. "Cowards and Heroes: Group Loyalty in the American Civil War." *Quarterly Journal of Economics* 118(2): 519-48.

–. 2006. "Forging a New Identity: The Costs and Benefits of Diversity in Civil War Combat Units for Black Slaves and Freemen." *Journal of Economic History* 66(4): 936-62.

Creswell, J.W. 2006. *Designing and Conducting Mixed Methods Research*. Thousand Oaks, CA: Sage.

Daftary, F., ed. 2011. *A Modern History of the Ismailis: Continuity and Change in a Muslim Community*. London: I.B. Tauris.

Dépelteau, F. 2008. "Relational Thinking: A Critique of Co-Deterministic Theories of Structure and Agency." *Sociological Theory* 26(1): 51-73.

Dewing, M. 2009. "Canadian Multiculturalism." Library of Parliament Background Paper No. 2009-20-E. Available at http://www.parl.gc.ca/Content/LOP/Research Publications/2009-20-e.htm.

DeYoung, C.P., M.O. Emerson, G. Yancey, and K.C. Kim. 2005. "All Churches Should be Multiracial: The Biblical Case." *Christianity Today*, 32-35.

Dixon, J.C. 2006. "The Ties That Bind and Those That Don't: Toward Reconciling Group Threat and Contact Theories of Prejudice." *Social Forces* 84(4): 2179-204.

Dossa, P. 2009. *Racialized Bodies, Disabling Worlds: Storied Lives of Immigrant Muslim Women*. Toronto: University of Toronto Press.

Durkheim, É. 2006 [1897]. *On Suicide*. Toronto: Penguin.

Emerson, M.O., R.T. Kimbro, and G. Yancey. 2002. "Contact Theory Extended: The Effects of Prior Racial Contact on Current Social Ties." *Social Science Quarterly* 83(3): 745-61.

Eng, L.A. 2002. *Report on IPS Research Forum on Ethnic Relations in Singapore, 24 Oct 2002*. Singapore: The Institute of Policy Studies. Accessed at http://www.spp.nus.edu.sg/ips/docs/ reports/ rp_erpforumreport.pdf.

Esposito, J.L., and D. Mogahed. 2007. *Who Speaks for Islam? What a Billion Muslims Really Think*. New York: Gallup Press.

Fatah, T. 2010. *The Jew Is Not My Enemy: Unveiling the Myths That Fuel Muslim Anti-Semitism*. Toronto: McClelland and Stewart.

Fox News. 2012. "Focus: Stop All Muslim Immigration." Panel discussion. Available at http://www.youtube.com/watch?v=VUDjMn9oDmk.

Gans, H.J. 1992. "Second-Generation Decline: Scenarios for the Economic and Ethnic Futures of the Post-1965 American Immigrants." *Ethnic and Racial Studies* 15(2): 173-92.

Geertz, C. 1973. *The Interpretation of Cultures*. New York: Basic Books.

GhaneaBassiri, K. 2010. *A History of Islam in America*. New York: Cambridge University Press.

Gualtieri, A. 2004. *The Ahmadis: Community, Gender, and Politics in a Muslim Society*. Montreal and Kingston: McGill-Queen's University Press.

Haile, D., A. Sadrieh, and H.A. Verbon. 2008. "Cross-Racial Envy and Under-investment in South Africa." *Cambridge Journal of Economics* 32(5): 703-24.

Hamdani, D.H. 1999. "Canadian Muslims on the Eve of the Twenty-First Century." *Journal of Muslim Minority Affairs* 19(2): 197.

Harris, S. 2004. *The End of Faith: Religion, Terror, and the Future of Reason*. New York: Norton.

Harris, S. 2012. "Islam and the Future of Liberalism." Available at http://www. samharris.org/blog/item/islam-and-the-future-of-liberalism.

Hashemi, N. 2009. *Islam, Secularism, and Liberal Democracy: Toward a Democratic Theory for Muslim Societies.* New York: Oxford Univeristy Press.

Hirji, F. 2011. "Through the Looking Glass: Muslim Women on Television – An Analysis of *24, Lost,* and *Little Mosque on the Prairie." Global Media Journal* 4(2): 33-47.

Hirsi Ali, A. 2010. *Nomad: From Islam to America.* New York: Free Press.

Howard, J.A. 2000. "Social Psychology of Identities." *Annual Review of Sociology* 26(1): 367-93.

Huber, G.A. and T.J. Espenshade. 1997. "Neo-Isolationism, Balanced-Budget Conservatism, and the Fiscal Impacts of Immigration." *International Migration Review* 31(4): 1031-54.

Hunter, S.T., ed. 2002. *Islam, Europe's Second Religion: The New Social, Cultural, and Political Landscape.* Westport, CT: Praeger.

Huntington, S.P. 1996. *The Clash of Civilizations and the Remaking of World Order.* New York: Simon and Schuster.

–. 2005. *Who Are We?* New York: Simon and Schuster.

Hurd, E.S. 2008. *The Politics of Secularism in International Relations.* Princeton: Princeton University Press.

Intelligence Squared, prod. 2010. *Islam Is a Religion of Peace.* Available at http:// www.youtube.com/watch?v=rh34Xsq7D_A

Jiwani, Y. 2006. *Discourses of Denial: Meditations of Race, Gender, and Violence.* Vancouver: UBC Press.

Johnson, R.B., and A.J. Onwuegbuzie. 2004. "Mixed Methods Research: A Research Paradigm Whose Time Has Come." *Educational Researcher* 33(7): 14-26.

Kadir, S. 2005. "The Role of Education in Ethnic/Religious Conflict Management: The Singapore Case." *ICIP Journal* 2(1): 1-18.

Kalin, I. 2011. "Islamophobia and the Limits of Multiculturalism." In J.L. Esposito and I. Kalin, eds., *Islamophobia: The Challenge of Pluralism in the 21st Century,* 3-20. New York: Oxford University Press.

Kanter, R.M. 1977. "Some Effects of Proportions on Group Life: Skewed Sex Ratios and Responses to Token Women." *The American Journal of Sociology* 82(5): 965-90.

Karim, K.H. 2003. *Islamic Peril: Media and Global Violence.* Montreal: Black Rose.

–. 2008. "Islamic Authority: Changing Expectations among Canadian Muslims." In N. Bakht, ed., *Belonging and Banishment: Being Muslim in Canada,* 85-98. Toronto: TSAR Publications.

–. 2011. "At the Interstices of Tradition, Modernity nad Postmodernity: Ismailie Engagements with Contemporary Canadian Society." In F. Daftary, ed., *A Modern History of the Ismailis: Continuity and Change in a Muslim Community,* 265-96. London: I.B. Tauris Publishers.

Kazemipur, A. 2006. "A Canadian Exceptionalism? Trust and Diversity in Canadian Cities." *Journal of International Migration and Integration* 7(2): 219-40.

–. 2009. *Social Capital and Diversity: Some Lessons from Canada.* Bern: Peter Lang.

–. 2012. "Employment and Social Integration of Immigrants: The Intersections with Gender and Religion." Paper presented at the research symposium entitled "Atlantic Canada: A Home Away from Home? Gender and Intersectional Perspectives on Immigration." St. John's, NL, September 28-29.

Kazemipur, A., and S.S. Halli. 2000. *The New Poverty in Canada: Ethnic Groups and Ghetto Neighbourhoods*. Toronto: Thompson Educational Publishing Inc.

Khan, A.Z. 2008. "Muslim Girl Magazine: Representing Ourselves." In N. Bakht, ed., *Belonging and Banishment: Being Muslim in Canada*. Toronto: TSAR Publications.

Kymlicka, W. 1989. *Liberalism, Community and Culture*. Oxford: Clarendon Press.

–. 1995. *Multicultural Citizenship*. New York: Oxford University Press.

–. 2005. "The Uncertain Futures of Multiculturalism." *Canadian Diversity*, 4(1): 82-85.

–. 2009. "The State of Multiculturalism in Canada." Paper presented at "Rethinking Identities in Contemporary Canada," Congress of the Humanities and Social Sciences, Ottawa, Canada, 27 May.

–. 2010. "Testing the Liberal Multiculturalist Hypothesis: Normative Theories and Social Science Evidence." *Canadian Journal of Political Science/Revue canadienne de science politique* 43(2): 257-71.

Kymlicka, W., and K. Banting. 2006. "Immigration, Multiculturalism, and the Welfare State." *Ethics and International Affairs* 20(3): 281-304.

Leuprecht, C., and C. Winn. 2011. *What Do Muslim Canadians Want? The Clash of Interpretations and Opinion Research*. Ottawa: The Macdonald-Laurier Institute.

Lewis, B. 1987. *Islam: From the Prophet Muhammad to the Capture of Constantinople*. Vol. 1: *Politics and War*. New York: Oxford University Press.

–. 2002. *What Went Wrong? Western Impact and the Middle Eastern Response*. New York: Oxford University Press.

Lucassen, L. 2005. *The Immigrant Threat: The Integration of Old and New Migrants in Western Europe since 1850*. Urbana: University of Illinois Press.

Manji, I. 2005. *The Trouble with Islam Today: A Muslim's Call for Reform in Her Faith*. New York: St. Martin's Griffin.

Mansur, S. 2009. *Islam's Predicament: Perspectives of a Dissident Muslim*. Oakville, ON: Mosaic Press.

Marschall, M.J., and D. Stolle. 2004. "Race and the City: Neighborhood Context and the Development of Generalized Trust." *Political Behavior* 26(2): 125-53.

Marx, A.W. 2003. *Faith in Nation: Exclusionary Origins of Nationalism*. New York: Oxford University Press.

Mata, F. 2011. "Religion-Mix Growth in Canadian Cities: A Look at 2006-2031 Projections Data." Paper presented at the conference "Taking Stock of a Turbulent Decade and Looking Ahead: Immigration to North America 2000-2010," organized by the Western Centre for Research on Migration and Ethnic Relations and the Canada-US Institute, Western University, London, ON, April 28-30.

McGown, R.B. 1999. *Muslims in the Diaspora: The Somali Communities of London and Toronto*. Toronto: University of Toronto Press.

McGreevy, J.T. 2003. *Catholicism and American Freedom*. New York: Norton.

McLaren, L.M. 2003. "Anti-Immigrant Prejudice in Europe: Contact, Threat Perception, and Preferences for the Exclusion of Migrants." *Social Forces* 81(3): 909-36.

Modood, T. 2007. *Multiculturalism*. Cambridge: Polity Press.

Moghissi, H. 2003. "Diaspora of Islamic Cultures: Continuity and Change. *Refuge* 21(2): 114-19.

Moghissi, H., ed. 2009. *Muslim Diaspora: Gender, Culture and Identity*. London: Routledge.

Moghissi, H., S. Rahnema, and M.J. Goodman. 2009. *Diaspora by Design: Muslim Immigrants in Canada and Beyond*. Toronto: University of Toronto Press.

Moody, J. 2001. "Race, School Integration, and Friendship Segregation in America." *American Journal of Sociology* 107(3): 679-716.

Municipalité-Hérouxville. 2010. Herouxville Town Charter. 16 April. Available at http://herouxville-quebec.blogspot.ca.

Nesbitt-Larking, P. 2008. "Dissolving the Diaspora: Dialogical Practice in the Development of Deep Multiculturalism. *Journal of Community and Applied Social Psychology* 18(4): 351-62.

Norton, Anne. 2013. *On the Muslim Question*. Princeton, NJ: Princeton University Press.

Oreopoulos, P. 2009. "Why Do Skilled Immigrants Struggle in the Labor Market? A Field Experiment with Six Thousand Résumés." Working Paper Series. Available at http://mbc.metropolis.net/assets/uploads/files/wp/2009/WP09-03.pdf.

Orwin, C. 2009. "Canadian Values Boil Down to Liberal Democracy." *Globe and Mail*, 9 April.

Persad, J.V. and S. Lukas. 2002. *"No Hijab Is Permitted Here": A Study on the Experiences of Muslim Women Wearing Hijab Applying for Work in Manufacturing, Sales and Service Sectors*. Report prepared for Women Working with Immigrant Women, December. http://atwork.settlement.org/downloads/no_hijab_is_permitted _here.pdf.

Perry, P., and A. Shotwell. 2009. "Relational Understanding and White Antiracist Praxis." *Sociological Theory* 27(1): 33-49.

Pettigrew, T.F. 1998. "Intergroup Contact Theory." *Annual Review of Psychology* 49(1): 65-85.

Pettigrew, T.F., and L.R. Tropp. 2006. "A Meta-Analytic Test of Intergroup Contact Theory." *Journal of Personality and Social Psychology* 90(5): 751-83.

Pew Research Center. 2007. *Muslim Americans: Middle Class and Mostly Mainstream*. http://pewresearch.org/pubs/483/muslim-americans.

–. 2011. *The Future of the Global Muslim Population: Projections for 2010-2030*. Report by Pew Research Center's Forum on Religion and Public Life, Washington, DC. http:// www.pewforum.org/files/2011/01/FutureGlobalMuslimPopulation-WebPDF-Feb10.pdf.

Porter, J. 1965. *The Vertical Mosaic: An Analysis of Social Class and Power in Canada*. Toronto: University of Toronto Press.

Powers, D.A., and C.G. Ellison. 1995. "Interracial Contact and Black Racial Attitudes: The Contact Hypothesis and Selectivity Bias." *Social Forces* 74(1): 205-26.

Putnam, R.D. 1994. *Making Democracy Work: ·Civic Traditions in Modern Italy*. Princeton: Princeton University Press.

–. 2001. *Bowling Alone: The Collapse and Revival of American Community*. New York: Simon and Schuster.

– 2007. "E Pluribus Unum: Diversity and Community in the Twenty-First Century: The 2006 Johan Skytte Prize Lecture. *Scandinavian Political Studies* 30(2): 137-74.

Putnam, R.D., D.E. Campbell. 2010. *American Grace: How Religion Divides and Unites Us*. New York: Simon and Schuster.

Ragin, C.C. 1987. *The Comparative Method: Moving beyond Qualitative and Quantitative Strategies*. Berkeley: University of California Press.

Ramadan, T. 2002. "Europeanization of Islam or Islamization of Europe?" In S.T. Hunter, ed., *Islam, Europe's Second Religion: The New Social, Cultural, and Political Landscape*, 207-18). Westport: Praeger.

–. 2004. *Western Muslims and the Future of Islam*. New York: Oxford University Press.

–. 2007. "Plotting the Future of Islamic Studies: Teaching and Research in the Current Political Climate." *Academic Matters*, December, 6-8.

–. 2010. *The Quest for Meaning: Developing a Philosophy of Pluralism*. London: Allen Lane (Penguin Books).

Rashid, R. 2011. *"Loneliness Is Killing Me": Life Stories and Experiences of Canadian Immigrant Women*. Lethbrdige, AB: University of Lethbridge Press.

Raza, M.M. 2012. "Social and Human Capital: The Determinants of Economic Integration of South Asian Immigrants in Canada." PhD diss., University of Western Ontario.

Razack, S. 2008. *Casting Out: The Eviction of Muslims from Western Law and Politics*. Toronto: University of Toronto Press.

Reitz, J.G. 2009a. "Assessing Multiculturalism as a Behavioural Theory." In J.G. Reitz, R. Breton, K.K. Dion and K.L. Dion, eds., *Multiculturalism and Social Cohesion: Potentials and Challenges of Diversity*, 1-47. New York: Springer.

–. 2009b. "Multiculturalism and Social Cohesion: Potentials and Challenges of Diversity." Paper presented at the *Armchair Discussions*, organized by the Metropolis Project. Ottawa, June 11. http://canada.metropolis.net/events/armchairs_e.html.

Reitz, J.G., R. Breton, K.K. Dion, and K.L. Dion. 2009. *Multiculturalism and Social Cohesion: Potentials and Challenges of Diversity*. New York: Springer.

Sacerdote, B., and D. Marmaros. 2005. *How Do Friendships Form?* NBER Working Paper No. 11530 Cambridge: National Bureau of Economic Research. Available at http://www.nber.org/papers/w11530.pdf?new_window=1.

Said, E. 1979. *Orientalism*. New York: Vintage.

Sanchez, G.J. 1997. "Face the Nation: Race, Immigration, and the Rise of Nativism in Late Twentieth Century America." *International Migration Review* 31(4): 1009-30.

Sanders, J.M. 2002. "Ethnic Boundaries and Identity in Plural Societies." *Annual Review of Sociology* 28(1): 327-57.

Satzewich, V., and L. Wong, eds. 2006. *Transnational Identities and Practices in Canada*. Vancouver: UBC Press.

Saunders, D. 2012a. "Muslims among Us: What the New Wave of Muslim Immigrants Can Teach Us about Uur Capacity for Fear." *Globe and Mail*, 25 August.

–. 2012b. *The Myth of the Muslim Tide: Do Immigrants Threaten the West?* New York: Vintage.

Schnall, S., J. Haidt, G.L. Clore, and A.H. Jordan. 2008. "Disgust as Embodied Moral Judgment." *Personality and Social Psychology Bulletin* 34(8): 1096-109.

Sen, A. 2006. *Identity and Violence: The Illusion of Destiny*. London: Norton.

–. 2009. *The Idea of Justice*. Cambridge: Harvard University Press.

Siddiqui, H. 2008. "Muslims and the Rule of Law." In N. Bakht, eds., *Belonging and Banishment: Being Muslim in Canada*, 1-16. Toronto: TSAR Publications.

Sigelman, L., T. Bledsoe, S. Welch, and M.W. Combs. 1996. "Making Contact? Black-White Social Interaction in an Urban Setting." *American Journal of Sociology* 101(5): 1306-32.

Sigelman, L., and S. Welch. 1993. "The Contact Hypothesis Revisited: Black-White Interaction and Positive Racial Attitudes." *Social Forces* 71(3): 781-95.

Simon, P., V.S. Pala. 2010. "We're Not All Multiculturalists Yet: France Swings between Hard Integration and Soft Anti-Discrimination." In S. Vertovec and S. Wessendorf, eds., *The Multiculturalism Backlash: European Discourses, Policies, and Practices*, 92-110. London: Routledge.

Soroush, A. 2002. *Reason, Freedom, and Democracy in Islam*. New York: Oxford University Press.

Stark, R., and W.S. Bainbridge. 1987. *A Theory of Religion*. New York: Peter Lang.

Stark, R., and R. Finke. 2000. *Acts of Faith: Explaining the Human Side of Religion* Berkeley: University of California Press.

Statistics Canada. 2001. 2001 Census Standard Data Products. Available at http://www.statcan.gc.ca/start-debut-eng.html.

–. 2005. Population by religion, by province and territory (2001 Census). Available at http://www.statcan.gc.ca/tables-tableaux/sum-som/l01/cst01/demo30c-eng.htm.

–. 2009. *Income in Canada: 2007*. Available at http://www.statcan.gc.ca/pub/75-202-x/75-202-x2010000-eng.htm.

Stein, R., S.S. Post, and A.L. Rinden. 2000. "Reconciling Context and Contact Effects on Racial Attitudes." *Political Research Quarterly* 53(2): 10.

Taylor, C. 1992. "The Politics of Recognition." In A. Gutman, ed., *Multiculturalism and the "Politics of Recognition,"* 25-74. Princeton: Princeton University Press.

–. 1994. *Multiculturalism and "the Politics of Reconstruction."* Princeton, NJ: Princeton University Press.

Teddlie, C., and A. Tashakkori. 2009. *Foundations of Mixed Methods Research: Integrating Quantitative and Qualitative Approaches in the Social and Behavioral Sciences*. Thousand Oaks, CA: Sage.

Tepperman, L., and Wilson, S.J. 1996. *Choices and Chances: Sociology for Everyday Life*. Toronto: Westview Press.

Tilly, C. 1984. *Big Structures, Large Processes, Huge Comparisons*. New York: Russell Sage Foundation.

–. 1998. *Durable Inequality*. Berkeley: University of California Press.

–. 2006. *Identities, Boundaries, and Social Ties.* Boulder: Paradigm.

–. 2007. *Democracy.* Cambridge: Cambridge University Press.

TVO 2011. "The Mosaic in Meltdown?" *The Agenda with Steve Paikin.* 1 February. Television interview available at http://www.youtube.com/watch?v=iCCKuZuBOkU.

Varshney, A. 2001. "Ethnic Conflict and Civil Society: India and Beyond." *World Politics* 53(3): 362-98.

Verkuyten, M. 2005. "Immigration Discourses and Their Impact on Multiculturalism: A Discursive and Experimental Study." *British Journal of Social Psychology* 44(2): 223-40.

–. 2007. "Religious Group Identification and Inter-Religious Relations: A Study among Turkish-Dutch Muslims." *Group Processes and Intergroup Relations* 10(3): 341-57.

Verkuyten, M., and B. Kinket. 2000. "Social Distances in a Multi Ethnic Society: The Ethnic Hierarchy among Dutch Preadolescents." *Social Psychology Quarterly* 63(1): 75-85.

Verkuyten, M., and B. Martinovic. 2006. "Understanding Multicultural Attitudes: The Role of Group Status, Identification, Friendships, and Justifying Ideologies." *International Journal of Intercultural Relations* 30: 1-18.

Verkuyten, M., and J. Thijs. 2002. "Multiculturalism among Minority and Majority Adolescents in the Netherlands." *International Journal of Intercultural Relations* 26: 91-108.

Vigdor, J.L. 2011. *Comparing Immigrant Assimilation in North America and Europe*: New York: Manhattan Institute for Policy Research.

Webb, J., T. Schirato, and G. Danaher. 2002. *Understanding Bourdieu.* Thousand Oaks, CA: Sage.

Wilders, G., prod. 2011. "Deporting Millions of Muslims May Be Necessary." Video clip available at http://www.youtube.com/watch?v=Rfm1l9g8UAY.

Wilson, W.J. 1987. *The Truly Disadvantaged: The Inner City, the Underclass, and Public Policy.* Chicago: University of Chicago Press.

–. 1997. *When Work Disappears: The World of the New Urban Poor.* New York: Vintage.

Wingrove, J. 2010. "Naheed Nenshi Becomes Canada's First Muslim Mayor." *Globe and Mail,* 19 October. Available at http://www.theglobeandmail.com/news/politics/calgarys-naheed-nenshi-becomes-canadas-first-muslim-mayor/article 1762765/page2/.

Wuthnow, R. 2002. "Bridging the Privileged and the Marginalized?" In R.D. Putnam, ed., *Democracies in Flux: The Evolution of Social Capital in Contemporary Society,* 59-102. New York: Oxford University Press.

Yancey, G. 1999. "An Examination of the Effects of Residential and Church Integration on Racial Attitudes of Whites." *Sociological Perspectives* 42(2): 279-304.

Young, L.A., ed. 1997. *Rational Choice Theory and Religion.* New York: Routledge.

Zhou, M. 1997. "Segmented Assimilation: Issues, Controversies, and Recent Research on New Second Generation." *International Migration Review* 31(4): 975-1008.

Zine, J. 2008. *Canadian Islamic Schools: Unravelling the Politics of Faith, Gender, Knowledge, and Identity.* Toronto: University of Toronto Press.

Index

f = figure / t = table

Printed and bound in Canada by Friesens

Set in Segoe and Warnock by Artegraphica Design Co Ltd.

Copy editor: Joanne Richardson

Proofreader and indexer: Dianne Tiefenesee